So Many
Leaders
...So Little
Leadership

Dr. John W. Stanko

Evergreen
PRESS

OTHER BOOKS BY JOHN STANKO:

Life Is a Gold Mine: Can You Dig It?
A Daily Dose of Proverbs
I Wrote This Book On Purpose...So You Can Know Yours

So Many Leaders...So Little Leadership
by John Stanko

ISBN 1-58169-048-7
For Worldwide Distribution. Printed in the U.S.A.

Evergreen Press
P.O. Box 91011 • Mobile, AL 36691 • 800-367-8203
E-mail: EvergreenBooks@aol.com

TABLE OF CONTENTS

DEDICATION

To Charles Simpson and all my friends and leaders
of the Covenant Church Movement,
whose courage to try new things was instrumental
in my leadership training.

INTRODUCTION

In first grade, I was the tallest student in my class. During gym class, the teacher would have us line up by height, and that put me first in line. We would then make a right face and run laps around the gymnasium. Pity the poor student who tried to pass me, as slow as I was. I would trip or grab them because, after all, it wasn't right for them to pass me—*I was the leader,* at least in that situation. Couldn't they see that? It was ordained by God, simple as that—or so I thought.

As I progressed through school, I didn't lack for leadership opportunities. I was in student council, generally leader of any sports team I was on (not based on talent; I simply wouldn't settle for anything less), and head of my prep school junior and senior class. I was first-chair violin in the orchestra and graduated first in my class. I was still the tallest, and that put me "head and shoulders" above my peers. It seemed to me that I was a born leader, and I enjoyed it.

I went to college and continued my propensity to lead. I was president of my fraternity, graduated in the top 10% of my class, and was accepted into Harvard's MBA program. At that point, I wanted to be a politician and lead from a position of political power. True to form, I won my first public election as a commissioner for the Model Cities program, one of President Lyndon Johnson's programs that was supposed to eradicate poverty. But a funny thing happened on my way to political leadership.

Before I could take my seat as a Model Cities commissioner, I had to withstand a challenge from the African American community. Due to a technicality regarding my residency, a judge threw out the results of my election. I lost the second election by nine votes! I was crushed.

But that setback was one of the best things that ever happened to me. During that time, I met some people who talked to me about my relationship with the Lord. I had to admit that I didn't have much of one, although I had dutifully followed the directives of my denomination. On May 18, 1973, while a graduate student at Duquesne University in Pittsburgh, I prayed a prayer and yielded my life to God. My life has never been the same, and neither has my "call" to leadership.

True to course, I started and led a Bible study on campus, and it grew. But I expected that—I was a *leader*! But the Lord was about to teach me lessons that would change the course of my life, and alter my understanding of my leadership and leadership in general. Those lessons all had the same conclusion: A price has to be paid to become an effective leader. I learned that leadership isn't something that just happens or comes "naturally."

This book will explain some of the lessons I've learned over the last 25 years that I've served as a leader.

Now I know what you're thinking—you don't need another book on leadership. And you may be right! The market, both Christian and secular, is full of titles about leadership style and preparation, and many of them have good things to say. I know because I've read a lot of them. The fact that there *are* already a lot of books on leadership, however, is a good reason to write another one.

I want to talk to you in this book about the issues that are dear to me, ones that have enhanced my leadership abilities and style. In 1991, I began to talk to groups of people about finding their life purpose. That message is as fresh today as it was in 1991. I want to help you establish your leadership on a firm foundation of purpose and then see you set goals and manage your life and time from that focus.

Leaders need constant input to help them grow and develop. Leaders and potential leaders are (or should be) hungry to learn, grow, and be more effective at what they do. Not only that, but the modern age is putting demands on leaders like never before. Changes in technology and the global marketplace increase pressure on leaders to react quickly and correctly. A leadership mistake today can cost an organization its very existence. Thus I'm encouraged to write and add my own insights and experiences to the body of leadership knowledge that already exists.

But I have other reasons for writing this book. The title— *So Many Leaders, So Little Leadership*—may give you a clue. I'm writing because I'm concerned about the lack of *effective* leadership that I find in the world today, whether in the church, politics, education, or business. I've observed firsthand the tendency toward heavy-handed, authoritarian leadership styles that discourage and confuse those who are following. A leader once told me that authority is like a bar of soap: the more you use it, the less you have. Some leaders are about "washed up," if that statement holds true.

Robert Greenleaf is an author who has deeply impacted my life lately. He's no longer alive, but his writings have a greater significance today than ever before. I'll refer to him quite often as we go along. He wrote:

> We live amid a pervasive leadership crisis. It is a crisis without precedent, and it affects all dimensions of life. There have always been and probably always will be

leaders, persons who are most able to foresee where to go, who are willing to take the risks of going out ahead to show the way, and who are trusted by those who follow them. People have been poorly served before, as many are now, by those whose leadership they choose to follow. What is different in our times is that, in the past hundred years, we have moved from a society of artisans, farmers, merchants, and professionals, with small government and military, to widespread involvement with a vast array of institutions—often large, complex, powerful, impersonal, not always competent, and sometimes corrupt. There is nothing like it in our history. Recent experience with these institutions has brought a new awareness of serious deficiencies in our common life that are clearly traceable to leadership inadequacies that result in these institutions' both serving poorly and hurting people.

Part of this leadership failure can be attributed to the predominance of coercion within our institutions, and this may in turn be due to the failure of so many who could persuade, and who might lead more fulfilled lives as persuaders, to make their influence felt in the leadership of institutions. Some resources have long been, and may always be, devoted to rescuing people from the hurt of "the system," wherever it happens to be. But in our day, some of these institutions are grinding people down faster than the most valiant efforts can recover them. Some of the effort now devoted to caring for the hurt of people should be diverted to caring for institutions, with a prime concern for how they are structured and how they are led.[1]

I've seen many leaders act in a manner that protects their own self-interests in the short-run, and that has damaged the organization they were leading in the long-run. Harriett Tubman wrote a fascinating book entitled *The March of Folly*. In it, she outlines historical examples of how leaders have made decisions that cost their organizations and countries dearly, even though they had information and advice that their decisions were the wrong ones! These leaders just couldn't bring themselves to overcome pride, public opinion and pressure, or their own fears to act and lead in the best interests of those they were leading. So many leaders, so little leadership.

In addition to poor leadership, it saddens me that many leaders haven't paid the price to become the leader that they could or should be. Instead of developing leadership skills, too often they have relied on charisma, giftedness, manipulation, control, or anger to lead people. I've been guilty of this as well, and I'm still learning how to lead without overwhelming or manipulating those who follow. I'm also still learning that I exist to *serve the organizations* I lead and not the other way around. It's not easy. But that doesn't mean it can't or shouldn't be done.

I offer this book in the hope that the emerging generation of leaders will learn a better way. I also hope that existing leaders will adjust their styles to incorporate a more balanced approach. I'm *not* against strong leadership, but strong leadership is called to serve people and causes, not themselves. This may be the greatest price that a leader must pay—to sacrifice personal interests for corporate ones; to give away the power that leadership brings to those who follow. Jesus warned His leaders not to be like the Gentile leaders who lord it over those they are leading (see Luke 22:24-26). This doesn't pertain only to "religious" leaders but to *all* leaders.

Since my conversion in 1973, I've studied the Bible, earning a doctorate in pastoral ministries along the way. I've led secular and religious organizations. I've read hundreds of management and leadership books, but I've always returned to the Bible as my ultimate source of insight and as a standard to evaluate what I've read and studied.

I've found, as others have, that the Bible is full of leadership stories and principles. I've been intrigued lately at how many leadership experts quote the Bible. I'm going to "join the crowd" and draw heavily from the Old and New Testaments in a way that I trust will be enlightening and "non-religious." My hope is to expose the reader who isn't familiar with the Bible to some timeless wisdom on the subject of leadership.

At the same time, I'll quote from leadership sources that may or may not be Christian in their approach or mindset, but who have valuable insights into the world of leadership—writers such as Stephen Covey, Max DePree, Peter Drucker, Robert Greenleaf, Warren Bennis, and Noel Tichy. By doing this, I want to expose the Christian reader to some good material that he or she may not be familiar with. After all, truth is truth, no matter where you find it.

And finally, I'll talk about my own journey, drawing on stories and experiences that have been meaningful to my own leadership development. I humbly offer these not as an expert, but as one who was born to lead *and* who has worked to become the best leader that I can be by God's grace. I admit that I'm still learning, and I have a long way to go. But today, I want more than ever to be a leader whom God uses and people follow, so with that in mind, I would like to acknowledge some people who have impacted my life and leadership style over the years.

First, there was my first supervisor, Dr. Joseph Merante,

former director of admissions at the University of Pittsburgh. Dr. Merante taught me how to release someone to their leadership development when he released me at a time when he still needed me. He paid a price. He confronted me and caused some major attitudinal changes in my life and that took a lot of courage. Thanks, Dr. Merante.

Then there's Bishop Joseph Garlington, founder and pastor of Covenant Church of Pittsburgh, my pastor, mentor, and friend. We have been together for 25 years, and his leadership style has affected me greatly. He has invested heavily in my development, and I'll always be grateful for that and mindful that I must bring a return on his investment. I know it hasn't been easy to work with me, Bishop Joseph, but thank you for everything.

Then there's Pastor Charles Simpson, former pastor of Covenant Church of Mobile in Alabama. Charles let me get close to him and his world, and that opportunity contributed more to my leadership philosophy than perhaps anything else. By allowing me to grow, make mistakes, and learn from those mistakes, Charles Simpson had a major impact on my life and leadership.

I haven't always agreed with everything that these leaders have done or how they did it. But that's part of the price of leadership, too—to have someone like me watching the one in charge and second-guessing their style and decisions. It was easy for me to do that because I didn't have the pressure of leadership and decision-making. As my leadership sphere increases, I appreciate all the more the job that these and other leaders have to do. And it is to these and *all* leaders that I dedicate this book.

Section One

PURPOSE, VALUES, PHILOSOPHY, INFLUENCE

People who reach exceptional heights may differ from each other, but one thing they all share is a clear goal born of some organizing purpose that summons their talents, aims their efforts, and steers them in the right direction. A compelling purpose is the ambitious person's true north, keeping him or her on course. What kind of purpose is worth pursuing? The most satisfying purpose empowers its pursuer to enlist others in a quest for some higher good.
—James Champy and Nitin Nohria,
The Arc of Ambition

Chapter One

LEADING FROM THE INSIDE OUT

As I write this first section, I'm sitting in a hotel room in Nakuru, Kenya, East Africa. I'm here to speak at a conference and to assess the current leadership team of a large church. This particular church is growing quickly, and many young men and women are being brought into leadership positions. I can already see the pressure they are under as they work to keep up with the growth and programs that this church has.

I'm convinced as I sit and talk with these leaders that the leadership call and journey starts from within. Yes, I know that leadership manifests itself when someone steps out in front of the crowd and the crowd follows. But I'm convinced that leaders must begin the journey to lead from within their own hearts.

Leadership isn't about techniques or training only. If leaders don't know who they are, insecurity and the need to stay on top will cause them to make unwise decisions, thus undermining the leadership they're trying to assert and establish. Or they'll work themselves too hard, trying to be all things to all people so as not to fail in their leadership role. I see this, especially the latter, as I work with these young leaders in Kenya.

As we begin, I want to review a concept from my previous books and introduce two new ones in the next two chapters that have helped me in my approach to leadership. Let's start with my favorite topic—your life purpose.

Everyone has a purpose in life. It may take some time to find or to fulfill, but it's there. In my book, *I Wrote This Book on Purpose . . . So You Can Know Yours*, I've presented many examples and exercises to help you clearly identify your purpose. Without a life purpose or mission statement, you'll be like a sailboat following the wind direction of the moment. Without a destination, any course will do.

In a later chapter, we'll look at one of the great historical leaders of the Judeo-Christian movement—Moses. The New Testament tells us that "Moses thought that his own people would realize that God was using him to rescue them, but they did not" (Acts 7:25). Moses knew what his purpose in life was—to rescue the Jews from Egypt. And he would do just that, but not until he went through 40 years of preparation. Yet knowing who he was and what he was to do kept him on course, even through the tough, lonely years. And when he finally fulfilled his purpose and led his people out, he was for the most part a model leader who combined strength and meekness, power and patience, action and prayer. More on him later.

Another leader we'll study was also an Old Testament hero—King David. When David was a boy, a prophet poured oil on him and anointed him as the successor to the reigning king, Saul. "And from that day on the Spirit of the Lord came upon David in power" (1 Samuel 16:13). David knew at a young age that he would be king. He just didn't know when or how it would come about.

Many years later, the tribes of Israel came to him and said, "The Lord said to you, 'You will shepherd my people Israel, and you will become their ruler'" (2 Samuel 5:2). David knew who he was and didn't exert power to overthrow the current king or to manipulate the political situation to his advantage. He waited, and his time came. He knew he was a leader who had to go through the preparation process before he was ready. In short, David knew his purpose.

If you don't know what your purpose is, then you'll always be insecure in your leadership. You'll worry about becoming or staying a leader. And that may cause you to use people for your own ends or make decisions to protect what you have. If you know that you have a divine destiny, then you can lead without fear! You can make hard decisions, knowing that your leadership is rooted in something deeper than public opinion, the board of directors' vote, or the stock price of your company. Your leadership will be rooted in your heart and only you (and God) can touch it there.

My life purpose, as I explain in my previous books, is "to bring order out of chaos." This is my purpose statement:

MY LIFE'S PURPOSE

I surrendered my life to Jesus Christ on May 18, 1973. The next day I received His call to "give my life to full-time service." From that, I've come to realize that my life's purpose is to "bring order out of chaos" wherever the Lord chooses to send me. A verse to help define this purpose is found in Genesis 1:2:

Now the earth was formless and empty, darkness was over the surface of the deep, and the Spirit of God was hovering over the waters.

4

I know who I am. It's the foundation for my leadership. I've changed leadership positions many times over the last 20 years, but in each position, my purpose has been the same—to find the chaos, the potential, and bring order to it. I don't have a resumé, nor have I ever applied for a job in my 28-year career. God has made me a leader by who I am, not by what I can conquer or control. Yet most who know me would probably say that I'm a strong leader. Strength comes from knowing who you are and where the essence of your leadership comes from. I've learned to lead from the inside out.

You can't be the best leader possible if you are trying to be like someone else. You must be who you are—and be that to the fullest—if your leadership is ever to reach its maximum potential.

If you aren't sure about your purpose, then I refer you to my two books, *Life Is a Gold Mine: Can You Dig It?* and *I Wrote This Book on Purpose . . . So You Can Know Yours.* Both books provide helpful insights so that you can identify your purpose, and both books refer you to other authors who can do the same. Don't even think of leading without knowing your life's purpose. It will keep you focused, sane, and effective in the good times and the bad.

Chapter Two

DEFINING YOUR GOVERNING VALUES

In chapter one, I stated that leadership starts from within a man or woman. It's a heart matter. As I've studied successful leaders, I've seen that they have almost always developed an inner set of values, whether they are aware that they have or not. Each one has a set of guidelines that help them make decisions, small or great. Some have written down these values and carry them in a notebook or planner; others carry them on the "tablets of their heart." Most often these values were developed and defined from:

- Family examples, both positive and negative
- Mentoring relationships
- Religious teachings
- Life failures
- Suffering through tough times
- Watching other leaders whom they admired
- Watching other leaders whom they did not admire

For instance, some who were taken advantage of have vowed never to do the same, and others, out of the same situation, decided to take advantage of as many people as possible. Both have developed values that guide their decisions and develop their leadership style. Others have felt the pain of domineering leadership and decided to perpetuate that style; some hold the value not to rule with an iron fist, but rather with an open hand. Both have developed values. And without realizing it, you have developed some values, too.

Robert Greenleaf, in his book, *On Becoming a Servant Leader*, stated: "This is the ultimate test: what values govern one's life—at the end of it?"[2] He poses an interesting question, don't you think?

Are you developing a set of values that adjust over your lifetime as your leadership grows and matures? You shouldn't wait until you're a leader to try to define these values, for by then you may not see the importance of such a task ("I'm already a leader; why sweat the small stuff now when big decisions await?"). If you wait too long to reflect on your values, you may find that you've already given your energy to values that weren't worth the effort you gave them.

As most successful leaders, the Apostle Paul had a set of values that guided his ministry and ministry decisions:

1. Not taking financial support from the churches he was starting

2. Not working where someone had already labored to start a church

3. Always visiting the synagogue first when arriving in an area

4. Traveling in the company of a team

5. Not maintaining a Jewish lifestyle as he visited diverse cultures and people

Paul's success wasn't a matter of chance. At least part of his success came from the fact that he had a set of values that served to guide his life and work decisions. He didn't impose these values on others, for they belonged to him, having been shaped by his own experience and understanding of what God wanted him to do.

I'm grateful to the Franklin Covey Company for helping me develop my values. While studying to become a certified time management facilitator through that company, their instructor directed all those being trained to write out our values. He told us there weren't a maximum or minimum number, and he encouraged us to write them in a positive style that related to the present ("I am"), and not the future ("I will"). Then he asked that we attempt to prioritize those values and from that point forward carry them with us for regular review and adjustment.

The company's objective was to allow us to see our values and allow them to better guide our decisions, decisions we would be making as leaders. In fact, they called these values our *governing* values, since they do, sometimes without realizing it, govern our life and decisions. I have to say that this has been a most rewarding experience. I now regularly work with other leaders and potential leaders to help them develop a set of values that will guide (or are guiding) their life and leadership.

I offer my own set of values as an example of how they can be done, not as a model list of values to be held. I developed mine by identifying my favorite passages from the Bible. I then did what Franklin Covey asked me to do: I put some narrative explanation to each value and prioritized them.

Developing values, however, isn't a science with rigid rules and procedures; rather, it's an art. At the end of my list, I'll make some further recommendations of how to develop your list of governing values. Keep in mind that mine are based on a Christian life and worldview and aren't offered with anything in mind except to give you a better understanding of my leadership style and what updated, prioritized governing values can look like.

MY GOVERNING VALUES
(Updated April 6, 1999)

1. I do the will of God.

I prayed one time that I would be like Timothy, not fully realizing what I was praying. I saw Timothy in a whole new light as I read Philippians 2:19-23:

> *I hope in the Lord Jesus to send Timothy to you soon, that I also may be cheered when I receive news about you. I have no one else like him, who takes a genuine interest in your welfare. For everyone looks out for his own interests and not those of Jesus Christ. But you know that Timothy has proved himself, because as a son with his father he has served with me in the work of the gospel. I hope, therefore, to send him as soon as I see how things go with me.*

The will of God, as I understand it, is to put others' interests before my own and to *serve* in furthering the Gospel as the Holy Spirit and my oversight so direct. That also involves a vibrant and diligent prayer and study life that seeks to find the will of God and do it.

2. I walk in faith.

The writer of Hebrews wrote, "Without faith it is impossible to please God." I want to please the Lord by exercising faith in Him concerning my purpose, family, finances, future, and relationships. The second part of that verse completes the thought when it says, "because anyone who comes to him must believe that he exists and that he rewards those who earnestly seek him" (Hebrews 11:6).

My faith will have practical expression through my giving habits as I'm generous with my time, knowledge, wisdom, and money.

3. **I love my family**.

The Lord has given me three wonderful gifts: Kathryn, my wife, and my two children, John and Deborah. The Apostle Paul commanded husbands to love their wives...

> *...just as Christ loved the church and gave himself for her to make her holy, cleansing her by the washing with water through the word, and to present her to himself as a radiant Church, without stain or wrinkle or any other blemish, but holy and blameless. In the same way, husbands ought to love their wives as their own bodies* (Ephesians 5:25-28).

I want to love my wife and see her released to her purpose as a joint heir with me of the gracious gift of life (1 Peter 3:7).

He also told fathers not to "embitter your children, or they will become discouraged" (Colossians 3:21). I want to be a friend and encourager to my children and release them to their God-given purpose.

4. **I am a reconciler.**

The Gospel of Jesus Christ is the only answer to society's problems, and that includes racism. I offer myself to work with people of color and of various cultures to model relationships that will help reconcile people to God and then to one another. As Paul wrote in 2 Corinthians 5:18-20,

> *All this is from God, who reconciled us to himself through Christ and gave us the ministry of reconciliation; that God was reconciling the world to himself in Christ, not counting men's sins against them. And he has committed to us the message of reconciliation. We are therefore Christ's ambassadors, as though God were making his appeal through us. We implore you on Christ's behalf: Be reconciled to God.*

I want to mentor young men and women to equip them to be all that they can be in God and affirm their beauty and worth in God's eyes.

5. **I am a learner.**

Because the world is changing so rapidly, I can't afford to "crystallize" in my work habits or thinking. That means that I must continue to learn and grow in the knowledge of God (Colossians 1:10). My primary focus must be the Word of God, and my prayer is "open my eyes that I may see wonderful things in your law" (Psalm 119:18). Paul wrote that "all Scripture is God-breathed and is useful for teaching, rebuking, correcting and training in righteousness, so that the man of God may be thoroughly equipped for every good work" (2 Timothy 3:16).

I'll read, study, take classes, attend seminars, learn from role models, and master new techniques and technology that will enable me to learn until my strength fails or I die.

6. **I am a leader.**

Since my childhood, I've found myself in leadership positions. I want to be the kind of leader that God wants me to be by making decisions that are according to His will and implementing them in the right spirit and attitude. Peter wrote,

> *Be shepherds of God's flock that is under your care, serving as overseers—not because you must, but because you are willing, as God wants you to be; not greedy for money, but eager to serve; not lording it over those entrusted to you, but being examples to the flock* (1 Peter 5:2-3).

I want to lead in the tradition of Jesus, Moses, Joseph, David, Solomon, and Daniel. I want to be effective, pursue excellence, and be efficient as I lead and also reflect the Lord in my relationships. I also want to be a leader of integrity and courage.

7. **I am a team player.**

I've been an avid sports fan since my youth. I now realize that this was simply a love for the team concept that's so vital to, yet so absent from, much of management and ministry today. I want to help people identify their life's purpose and then train and coach them to work with other people of purpose. I'll try to pursue the synergy that comes from teamwork when everyone has a chance to communicate and share their creativity in an open atmosphere as free from authoritarian techniques as possible.

The Apostle Paul almost always traveled in a team and was released into ministry from the context of "team" in Acts 13:1-3:

> *In the church at Antioch there were prophets and teachers: Barnabas, Simeon called Niger, Lucius of Cyrene, Manaen (who had been brought up with Herod*

the tetrarch) and Saul. While they were worshiping the Lord and fasting, the Holy Spirit said, "Set apart for me Barnabas and Saul for the work to which I have called them." So after they had fasted and prayed, they placed their hands on them and sent them off.

8. **I am productive.**

The root word of executive is "execute." It's not enough to be busy, but I must execute correct plans and procedures that will produce the desired fruit and results. The writer of Hebrews cautioned,

> *Land that drinks in the rain often falling on it and that produces a crop useful to those for whom it is farmed receives the blessing of God. But land that produces thorns and thistles is worthless and is in danger of being cursed. In the end it will be burned* (Hebrews 6:7-8).

I want to produce more than I use and engage in activities that will bring increase and glory to God and to those with whom I'm working.

9. **I am a communicator.**

Jesus was a great communicator. Mark reported that "the large crowd listened to him [Jesus] with delight" (Mark 12:37). That came from His insight into the Word, His love for people, and His effective speaking style. I want to follow in His footsteps. Jesus also said, "The Father who sent me commanded me what to say and how to say it" (John 12:49).

I want to have something to say and then know how to present it with clarity, humor, and conviction, whether speaking or writing. I also want to learn new languages that will allow me to communicate God's truth to other cultures.

I realize that stating these values in the "I am" style may seem a bit presumptuous or arrogant. I'm not everything that I've written above. But I'm striving to embody those values, and that keeps me humble and ever seeking—two traits missing in some leaders I work with. I can never say I've arrived; that could cause me to take shortcuts or expect certain privileges that could lead to defective leadership.

Now how about you? Are you ready to spell out your governing values? Here are some other sample values that I've borrowed from Franklin Covey to help you get started.

- I seek excellence.
- I am competent.
- I serve others.
- I am frugal.
- I am generous.
- I seek truth.
- I am self-sufficient.
- I am innovative.

If you're ready, then follow these simple steps:

1. Set aside two hours.

2. Identify phrases that represent values that have directed your life up to this point.

3. Identify phrases that represent values you wish to incorporate in your life from this point forward.

4. Clarify those phrases and give them definition.

5. Are any of your values harmful to you or others? Do

they represent selfish or selfless behavior? You may want to eliminate any that are inconsistent with a lifestyle of love and service (more on this later).

6. Set them in order of priority. Relax! There's no wrong way to do this.

7. Carry them with you. Review them every six months and change as needed.

Armed with a purpose statement and a set of values, you're now ready for the third component of the successful leader: a leadership philosophy. Let's look at that concept next.

Chapter Three

DEVELOPING A LEADERSHIP PHILOSOPHY

I've already mentioned King David in chapter one. Life wasn't always good or fair to David. After he was anointed as the successor to King Saul, he was

- Ridiculed by his brothers
- Taken advantage of by those he worked for
- Threatened and pursued by the one he was to replace
- A fugitive, wrongly accused of disloyalty
- Leader to a band of outlaws and outcasts

Out of all this, David had a lot of time to decide what kind of leader he was going to be. Would he be like Saul, who was making his life miserable? Would he bide his time and then seize the opportunity to be an arrogant leader full of ambition and insecurity like his predecessor? Somewhere in David's journey, and we don't know where or when, he made up his mind *not* to be like King Saul.

David didn't wait until he *became* a leader to decide how he would lead. Instead he decided beforehand, and when he became king, he was a gracious, kind, and well-loved leader.

He wasn't perfect and he made mistakes, but his leadership philosophy carried him through, and today he's still a model leader for those who will study him.

Perhaps no story reveals that King David had a leadership philosophy better than one found in 2 Samuel 9:

> *David asked, "Is there anyone still left in the house of Saul to whom I can show kindness for Jonathan's sake?" Now there was a servant of Saul's household named Ziba. They called him to appear before David, and the king said to him, "Are you Ziba?" "Your servant," he replied. The king asked, "Is there no one still left of the house of Saul to whom I can show God's kindness?" Ziba answered the king, "There is still a son of Jonathan; he is crippled in both feet"* (2 Samuel 9:1-4).

The king had this remaining son brought to him.

> *"Don't be afraid," David said to him, "for I will surely show you kindness for the sake of your father Jonathan. I will restore to you all the land that belonged to your grandfather Saul, and you will always eat at my table"* (2 Samuel 9:7).

This story tells me that David had the values of loyalty, covenant-keeping, and kindness firmly in his heart and at the center of his leadership philosophy. David had suffered much at the hands of this man's grandfather, King Saul. It would have been easy to go on and ignore this remaining heir in light of all that had happened.

But King David had made a covenant, an agreement with Mephibosheth's father, Jonathan. That agreement was for friendship and goodwill. And even though Saul and Jonathan were dead, David's leadership philosophy was very much alive. He was now exercising that philosophy by doing good to someone who didn't even know him.

I also developed a leadership philosophy in my years before I ever led anything. Coming from my purpose and values, I decided what kind of leader I wanted to be. I present this philosophy to you for your consideration and encourage you to write your own, whether you are or will be a leader.

MY LEADERSHIP PHILOSOPHY

I was born to lead. But I must continue to work hard to be the best leader that I can possibly be. At the same time, I want to exercise a team approach to leadership that will value the input and worth of every individual. As a leader, I'll share finances, success, and credit with all those who contribute. I'll also serve others so that they can become all that God wants them to be.

My leadership philosophy tells you a lot about me and my conclusions about leadership. First, I think leaders are born *and* made. Everyone can *learn* leadership skills because everyone will lead something, some time in their life. But leaders are *born* to accomplish certain things. This birth doesn't lead them to easy street, but to a life of discipline and hard work.

I believe that no one leader can make the difference alone. It takes a lot of people around the leader to make it all happen. Warren Bennis in his book *Co-Leaders: The Power of Great Partnerships* has this to say about the strong, one-person leader scenario:

This book reflects our conviction that you must look beyond the Bill Gateses of the world to understand what will make organizations succeed in the new millennium.

18

In this first comprehensive study of co-leaders and their often quiet power, we challenge the time-honored notion that all great institutions are the lengthened shadows of a Great Man or Woman. It is a fallacy that dies hard. But if you believe, as we do, that the genius of our age is truly collaborative, you must abandon the notion that the credit for any significant achievement is solely attributable to the person at the top. We have long worshiped the imperial leader at the cost of ignoring the countless other contributors to any worthwhile enterprise. In our hearts we know that the world is more complex than ever and that we need teams of talent— leaders and co-leaders working together—to get important things done. The old corporate monotheism is finally giving way to a more realistic view that acknowledges leaders not as organizational gods but as the first among contributors. In this new view of the organization, co-leaders finally come into their own and begin to receive the credit they so richly deserve.[3]

I want to draw out and acknowledge *all* those who are around me when I lead; and I want to value, even celebrate, their contributions and input. I don't want to fall into the trap that I have or need to have all the answers.

How can I do this? By being a good listener, by fostering dialogue, by creating situations where people can speak openly and honestly without fear of reprisal, to name a few. But I can also put some dollars in people's pockets when they do a good job. And I can publicly acknowledge others and their contributions. All of these things can create a team and tell people they are valued, respected, and needed.

Finally, my philosophy tells you that I've learned something about leadership and service. That's why Robert

Greenleaf's writings on those two topics have touched me so deeply. It's not up to those *under* a leader to serve, but for leaders themselves to serve those who are around, no matter where they stand on the hierarchical chart. I must use my power in leadership to help others achieve their place and leadership power. More on that later.

How about you? Take some time and think about your leadership style. If you are leading, how would you define your leadership style and approach? If not, how do you want to be perceived when you eventually do lead? It doesn't have to be long or involved; it should simply incorporate a summary of what's important to you as a leader.

No philosophy is going to prepare you for everything that you'll face once you're a leader. Thinking about driving a car and driving a car are two different things. But before you ever drive a car, you can make certain decisions and develop certain values that you'll be able to apply no matter what you encounter. After that, you simply need experience.

It's the same with leadership. Give some thought to it now, even if you've been leading for quite a few years. It's not too late to adjust, and it's never too early to begin preparation. Spell out your leadership philosophy. Once you've done that, you're ready to move on from the private work of being a leader to the public role, whenever that takes place.

Review

Let's review some assignments that you've been given in this first section concerning the inward work of being a leader.

1. **Identify your purpose.** If you haven't already, begin the journey to find a phrase that explains the essence of who you are. Be as specific as possible. Listen to your inner voice for confirmation and direction. Also listen to what

people are telling you about yourself. What situations consistently present themselves to you without your looking for them? All these things are very often clues to finding and describing who you are.

2. **Define your values.** Take time to list and explain those things in life that are important to you. Evaluate what you have. Is being wealthy a value? It certainly can be. If it's on your list, is it truly a value worth pursuing? If you want to give large sums of money away (another value) to the poor or to certain causes (representing more values such as the environment, missionary groups, or college scholarship funds), then being wealthy is probably a legitimate value for you. If it's an end unto itself, then you may need to evaluate the legitimacy of a life given to that value. Work your way through what's important to you by defining the values that are probably already directing your decisions.

3. **Develop your leadership philosophy.** Can you find a few phrases that summarize your leadership style? If you can, then you have a leadership philosophy. If not, then you have work to do. My philosophy was pretty much set by the time I found myself in leadership positions. It was formed by watching leaders and carefully thinking who I was and wasn't. I also read as much as I could read about leaders, both past and present. My philosophy is very comfortable to me. It fits like a tailored suit of clothes. And yours should, too. Don't settle for a collection of trite phrases that tell what others say you should be. Rather, work to find your own identity and leadership style.

Once you have done these things, let's look at an important mindset of service and influence that every good leader must have.

Chapter Four

SERVANT LEADERS

In the last chapter, I outlined several key personal beliefs about leadership that have made their way into my leadership philosophy. They include:

1. Leaders are born *and* made.

2. Leadership requires a lot of hard work.

3. Effective leaders, if they are truly effective, are surrounded by good people.

4. Good leaders need to recognize and reward the good people around them.

5. Leaders are servants.

Let's look more closely at the fifth one: servant leaders. A number of years ago I read Max DePree's book, *Leadership Is an Art.* It remains today one of my favorite books on leadership. In that book, DePree makes one simple statement about leadership that I have quoted and meditated on in many settings:

> The first responsibility of a leader is to define reality. The last is to say thank you. In between the two, the leader must become a servant and a debtor.[4]

That summary is profound, and I have found it to be true in my own leadership opportunities again and again.

On the front end, I must define the borders and parameters for those following me. That includes defining: the job, its financial objectives, why it is being done, how it fits into the overall picture, and who will do it. At the conclusion, I must say "thank you." And I try to say it with words *and* cash. But in between those two "bookends," I'm indebted to those who are doing the work, and I must serve them in whatever way necessary so that they can do their job. It's so simple, yet so hard to do!

I find the issue of service one of the hardest concepts for leaders to grasp. Let's make it more personal—I find it the hardest to accomplish! For help with this, I've turned to the Bible for both perspective and assistance.

As I do, let me say that I'm impressed with how many management and leadership experts quote from the Bible. Their search for wisdom always seems to lead them there. Yet when I go to conferences and ask them for their church affiliation, many want to let me know right away that they are not "church people." I find it sad that their search for wisdom has led them to the source of wisdom, yet has not affected their personal lives.

I have no such dilemma. I'm one of those "church people" through and through. For me, the Bible isn't a source of truth. It's *the* source of truth, and I've found it always to be accurate, especially when it talks about humanity and the issues of life. Enough said. Now back to the issue of service.

In Luke 22, I find a fascinating story about service. Jesus is gathered in the upper room with His disciples for what is now known as the Last Supper.

> *Also a dispute arose among them as to which of them was considered to be greatest. Jesus said to them, "The kings of the Gentiles lord it over them, and those who exercise authority over them call themselves Benefactors. But you are not to be like that. Instead, the greatest among you should be like the youngest, and the one who rules like the one who serves. For who is greater, the one who is at the table or the one who serves? Is it not the one who is at the table? But I am among you as one who serves"* (Luke 22:24-27).

This isn't the first time that Jesus had this discussion about service with His followers. But even now, as He prepared for His death, He found it necessary to go over it one more time because they were arguing over who had the most significant ministry. He then went on to practice what He preached by giving His life for those same followers.

Service isn't easy, but it's what leaders must do if their leadership is to be complete. It requires humility and a firm grasp on purpose and values. Leaders who serve followers have found the way to prevent power from corrupting their leadership. They've also found a way to keep from manipulating and controlling followers. It's through the simple practice and mentality of service.

Robert Greenleaf wrote,

> The servant-leader is servant first. It begins with the natural feeling that one wants to serve. Then conscious choice brings one to aspire to lead. The best test is: do those served grow as persons? Do they, while being served, become healthier, wiser, freer, more autonomous, more likely themselves to become servants?[5]

The major objection to leaders being servants is generally rooted in something that sounds like this: "I'm not working for people; they are working for me. I won't and can't have employees telling me (leadership) what to do." This reveals a faulty understanding of servant leadership and a bit of insecurity as well.

To clarify this misconception, I turn to Ken Blanchard, well-known author of *One-Minute* management fame. He explains concerning traditional leadership,

> Most organizations are typically pyramidal in nature. Who is at the top of the organization? The chief executive officer, the chairman, the board of directors. Who is at the bottom? All the employees—the people who do the work. . . . The paradox is that the pyramid needs to be right side up or upside down depending on the task or role.

> It's absolutely essential that the pyramid stay upright when it comes to vision, mission, values, and setting major goals. Moses did not go up on the mountain with a committee. People look to leaders for direction, so the traditional hierarchy isn't bad for this aspect of leadership.

> Most organizations and managers get in trouble in the implementation phase of the leadership process. The traditional pyramid is kept alive and well. When that happens, who do people think they work for? The person above them. The minute you think you work for the person above you for implementation, you are assuming that person—your boss—is *responsible* and your job is being *responsive* to that boss and to his or her whims or wishes. As a result, all the energy in the

organization is moving up the hierarchy, away from customers and the frontline folks who are closest to the action.[6]

Blanchard's remedy is to turn the pyramid upside down for the implementation. He further explains,

> That creates a very different environment for implementation. If you work for your people, what is the purpose of being a manager? *To help them accomplish their goals.* Your job is to help them win.[7]

So leaders must serve the organization by setting the direction and then serve the employees and customers by equipping everyone that can help the organization accomplish its mission. This fits in perfectly with what Max DePree wrote. First, leaders define reality for the organization—that includes the vision, mission, and goals. When it's all over, the leader says "Thank you," because the leader is the caretaker for the organization. In between, *everything* is service—making sure the staff, volunteers, and customers have everything *they* need so the organization prospers.

When I traveled with the music team of Worship International, I had numerous opportunities to put this into practice. I determined where we would go, picked the team members, worked out the budget, and made sure all the details were covered (I did this with the help and input of a lot of good people). When we got to the concert site, I put on my servant's hat. I made airport runs, picked up the bottled water and air cargo, and did whatever needed to be done to make sure the event was a success.

On Saturday night, I personally handed out the paychecks (I always had them ready beforehand) and said thanks for a job well done. I then took everybody back to the airport to catch a plane home. I still try to take the same role in whatever project I find myself leading.

If you want to do some more study and reading on servant-leaders, then I highly recommend Robert Greenleaf's works, specifically:

- *On Becoming a Servant Leader*
- *Seeker and Servant: Reflections on Religious Leadership*
- *The Power of Servant Leadership*
- *Insights on Leadership*

All of the above books are edited by Larry C. Spears, who serves as the director for

The Greenleaf Center for Servant-Leadership
921 E. 86th Street, Suite 200
Indianapolis, IN 46240
(317) 259-1241 (Phone) • (317) 259-0560 (FAX)
www.greenleaf.org

The Greenleaf Center has annual conferences and training seminars, a resource catalog that contains the books mentioned above, and other programs to help us all understand the implications and strategies of servant leaders.

Chapter Five

INFLUENCE, NOT CONTROL

In the last chapter, we looked at the concept of servant leaders. Let's add one more basic element to our understanding of leadership: Leaders should *influence*, not *control*.

There's no question that a leader has power. I'm *not* advocating that a leader surrender that power, but rather that a leader use his or her power in a manner that benefits both those who follow as well as the organization that everyone, including the leader, is serving. In the example from my experience with Worship International, I was instrumental in taking our worship events to 19 nations in four years. I used my power to help us accomplish our mission, not to rule the musicians or build a personal ministry.

As I mentioned earlier, a pastor once told me that authority is like soap: the more you use it, the less you have. Too often, leaders succumb to the temptation to use power to achieve personal goals, or to get people to do what the leader wants, regardless of whether the follower's heart agrees.

We've already looked at one biblical passage that speaks about this issue—Luke 22:25: "The kings of the Gentiles lord it over them; and those who exercise authority over them call themselves Benefactors. But you are not to be like that."

In another relevant passage that we looked at in chapter two that is also appropriate for this chapter, the Apostle Peter says,

> *Be shepherds of God's flock that is under your care, serving as overseers—not because you must, but because you are willing, as God wants you to be; not greedy for money, but eager to serve;* not lording it over those entrusted to you, but being examples to the flock (1 Peter 5:2-3 emphasis added).

And the Apostle Paul wrote in his letter to Philemon this interesting appeal:

> *Therefore, although in Christ* I could be bold and order you to do what you ought to do, yet I appeal to you, *on the basis of love. I then, as Paul—an old man and now also a prisoner of Christ Jesus—I appeal to you for my son, Onesimus, who became my son while I was in chains. Formerly he was useless to you, but now he has become useful both to you and to me. I am sending him—who is my very heart—back to you. I would have liked to keep him with me so that he could take your place in helping me while I am in chains for the gospel.* But I did not want to do anything without your consent, so that any favor you do will be spontaneous and not forced (Philemon 8-14, emphasis added).

In each instance, Jesus, Peter, and Paul were addressing people in leadership. They were giving them a different way to lead, one that gave followers room to grow, make decisions, and respond to the will of God and leadership out of a willing heart. These men understood that, as the adage goes, "A man convinced against his will remains a man unconvinced."

Recently, a leader called a mandatory meeting that required a financial commitment on the part of many employees. There was no dialogue or discussion. It was a done deal. I had a chance to talk to several people involved. A friend of mine, one of the kindest, gentlest men I know, shared his concerns with me. He said, "John, something rose up in me when that order to participate was given. I wish I could feel like I was participating in the decision, and I think I would have done it. But I feel like I had no say or ownership in the decision and I find myself resenting it."

Now some may interpret this to mean that the employee had a bad attitude. But what he said had merit. As an employee or member of a team, *you* want to know that you had input in decisions, especially ones that involve a serious commitment of time, money, or energy.

In the Old Testament, there's a story involving the prophet Elijah and his initial contact with his successor, Elisha. It provides an example of a leader *influencing* followers and *not controlling* them.

Let me set the background for the story. Elijah was in a bad place. He had run from Jezebel, the queen who wanted to have him killed, and ended up hiding in a cave. There, the Lord spoke to him and asked him why he was hiding. Elijah responded, "I have been very zealous for the Lord God Almighty. The Israelites have rejected your covenant, broken down your altars, and put your prophets to death with the sword" (1 Kings 19:10). Because of these terrible conditions, Elijah was suffering from some sort of depression. The Lord "encouraged" him by giving him something to do:

The Lord said to him, "Go back the way you came, and go to the Desert of Damascus. When you get there, anoint Hazael king over Aram. Also anoint Jehu son of Nimshi king over Israel, and anoint Elisha son of Shaphat from Abel Mehoiah to succeed you as prophet" (1 Kings 19:15-16).

Now Elijah was on a mission from God. So he set out on his journey to find Elisha, his successor. What did he do? Did he come to Elisha and make a dramatic scene? Did he relate to Elisha all that God had said? Let's look at what he did.

So Elijah went from there and found Elisha son of Shaphat. He was plowing with twelve yoke of oxen, and he himself was driving the twelfth pair. Elijah went up to him and threw his cloak around him. Elisha then left his oxen and ran after Elijah. "Let me kiss my father and mother good-by," he said, "and then I will come with you." "Go back," Elijah replied. "What have I done to you?" (1 Kings 19:19-20).

This story impresses me every time I read it. Elijah, armed with "the word of the Lord," didn't use that word to "hit Elijah over the head." He just *touched* him with it, leaving room for Elisha to determine on his own what had happened and what his response was to be. I interpret this to be an example of a leader using influence but not control over someone who was to be a follower.

In my own leadership, I try to emulate this scenario. There are many times when I have strong feelings about what needs to happen in a certain situation. But I'm interested in building a team and also interested in reaching a consensus where people who are following me feel that they had a part to play in the decision.

So staff meetings that I moderate and facilitate are very open. I try to hear from everyone and then use my "power" to direct the conversation, keep it on track, make sure the more powerful communicators don't overwhelm the more timid ones, and then use creativity to summarize the discussions. Out of that, I work to set the direction that we should go in and then try to give people time to reflect on that direction to see if they have any further reservations. It's definitely more time-consuming and requires more patience, but in the long run, yields better results because the people affected have owner-ship in the decision and direction.

I've sat in hundreds of business meetings, both secular and religious, and have been told what to do and how to do it. Most of the time, my point of view was not asked for; and when it was, many times it was not followed if it differed from the leader's perspective, even when I had greater experience or ex-pertise. And it sometimes made me feel used and unappreci-ated—and a bit angry. Very often I've felt as if I wasn't given time to assimilate the direction that was imposed or handed down. I'm not saying that the direction was wrong or that I would have come to a different conclusion, but the leader defi-nitely "strong armed" the group (and me) into compliance. And I didn't—and still don't—like it. I'm not sure that anyone does, based on honest feedback I've received from many other followers.

Elijah "touched" Elisha and then walked away. We know that because Elisha had to run after him once he had been touched. Obviously, Elisha sensed some significance in that touch, for he went home, closed out his affairs there, and joined Elijah. As far as we know, Elijah never told him to do that.

More often than not, I've found that if I give followers room to respond to a decision and the will of leadership, they'll do so positively and in a mature manner. If they don't, then there may be a need to sit down privately with them for further dialogue and communication. If there are two parties in a larger group that get at cross-purposes, it's sometimes necessary to adjourn the meeting and meet with those two. I've been able to resolve most conflicts in that manner. But all the while I'm using my power to influence and not manipulate or control people. I want to use my bar of soap for the right things.

Dialogue is an important tool for the leader who wants to influence and not control.

> Every man is a potential adversary, even those whom we love. Only through dialogue are we saved from this enmity toward one another. Dialogue is to love what blood is to the body. Then the flow of blood stops, the body dies. When dialogue stops, love dies and resentment is born. But dialogue can restore a dead relationship. Indeed, this is the miracle of dialogue—it can bring a relationship into being, and it can restore again a relationship that has died. There is only one qualification to these claims for dialogue. It must be mutual and perceived from both sides, and the parties must pursue it relentlessly.[8]

I've found that there's a lot of creativity and innovation among followers. When I cut off dialogue or communication and don't give them a chance to speak even if they are mistaken or "venting" their frustration, then I may lose the creativity or perspective that the follower has.

Ken Blanchard talks of insight he picked up from a seeing-eye dog training school. He found that schools eliminate two types of dogs. The first group is understandable—dogs that are totally disobedient. But the second group that is disqualified is more of a surprise—dogs that are totally obedient! Schools want to train dogs that follow only the commands that make sense. If the master gives the command to step off the curb when the dog sees a car approaching, that dog is trained *not* to obey.

I want followers around me who will stop me from walking out in front of "oncoming cars" that I can't see. To get them, I must redirect some of my power as a leader to include them in the decision-making process and submit to their decisions when they are functioning in their area of expertise or anointing. I must promote dialogue wherever and whenever possible and appropriate.

Greenleaf developed the best concept of leaders using influence that I have found. Consider this passage from the book, *On Becoming a Servant Leader*:

> *Persuasion* involves arriving at a feeling of rightness about a belief or action through one's own intuitive sense. One takes an intuitive step, from the closest approximation to certainty that can be reached by conscious logic (which is sometimes not very close) to the state in which one may say with conviction, "This is where I stand!" The act of persuasion, thus defined, would help order logic and favor the intuitive step. But the person being persuaded must take that intuitive step alone, untrammeled by coercive or manipulative stratagems of any kind. Persuasion, on a critical issue, is a difficult, time-consuming process. It demands one of the most exacting of human skills.[9]

The latter statement explains why it's so hard (especially for people dealing with "God's things") to work at influence and not succumb to control—it takes time! Visionary leaders often see something so clearly that in their mind it already exists. They therefore feel that they must get everyone on board as quickly as possible, and that often leads to manipulative tactics. The fact that they didn't intend it to be manipulative doesn't make it any less so.

Greenleaf defines manipulation as "the process of guiding people into beliefs or actions that they do not fully understand and that may or may not be good for them." He goes on to more fully explain,

> Because they are recognized as being better than most at leading, showing the way, they [leaders] are apt to be highly intuitive. Thus leaders themselves, in their conscious rationalities, may not fully understand why they choose a given path. Yet our culture requires that leaders produce plausible, convincing explanations for the directions they take. Once in a while, they can simply say, "I have a hunch that this is what we ought to do." However, most of the time, rational justifications are demanded, and part of the successful leader's skill is inventing these rationalizations. They are necessary, but they are also useful because they permit, after the fact, the test of conscious logic that "makes sense" to both leaders and follower. But the understanding by the follower, if he or she is not to be manipulated, is not necessarily contained in this rationalization that makes sense. Because we live in a world that pretends a higher validity to conscious rational thinking in human affairs than is warranted by the facts of our existence, and because many sensitive people "know" this, manipulation hangs as a cloud over the relationship between leader and led almost everywhere.[10]

But it's hard for most leaders to deal with this "cloud," as Greenleaf calls it, and to be patient and allow their followers to work through issues just like the leader did, no matter what business they're in. The answer for Greenleaf is consensus, which is "a method of using persuasion [influence] in groups."[11] There are four skills involved with any leader who wants to build consensus so that followers feel some sense of ownership in a decision. They are:

1. **The leader must be able to articulate the issues or problem.** Patience is required for those who are slower to grasp the situation.

2. **The leader must be a good listener.** By being this, the leader sets an example that others will follow in listening to all points of view.

3. **The leader must be sensitive to the discussions and begin to use his or her power to steer the group to a solution or conclusion.**

4. **The leader may have to meet with one or more followers who are maintaining a firm position that seems to be against the general consensus of the group.** Several options are available, which include deciding not to decide, waiting, or then using power to break the logjam and resolve the issue at hand.

Remember that this style of consensus-building, influencing, persuasive leadership doesn't work in every situation. When there's a crisis, there's a need for strong, experienced leaders to exercise decisiveness as they steer the group or organization out of trouble. But even in that situation, there's generally more room for communication, input, and dialogue than is currently employed in many leadership circles.

If you are a leader or on your way to becoming one, I urge you to consider the content of this chapter closely. Commit yourself to be a man or woman of influence who will build people up and not tear them down. Become a person who serves the vision and the people committed to the vision, and takes every opportunity to communicate and listen. If you do, you'll be a leader whom God can use and people will follow— a leader like Moses.

Section Two

THE PRICE OF LEADERSHIP FOR MOSES

When a prophet of the Lord is among you,
I reveal myself to him in visions, I speak to him in dreams.
But this is not true of my servant Moses; he is faithful in
all my house. With him I speak face to face, clearly and
not in riddles; he sees the form of the Lord
(Numbers 12:6-8).

Chapter Six

SCHOOL DAYS, SCHOOL DAYS

In the next few chapters, we'll look at a great Old Testament leader—Moses. I'm not going to focus on Moses' life as described in the Old Testament or in the books that he wrote—the first five books of the Bible known as the Pentateuch. Instead let's look at a speech found in the New Testament that was delivered by Stephen, the first Christian martyr.

> *At that time Moses was born, and he was no ordinary child. For three months he was cared for in his father's house. When he was placed outside, Pharaoh's daughter took him and brought him up as her own son. Moses was educated in all the wisdom of the Egyptians and was powerful in speech and action* (Acts 7:20-22).

Moses' parents saw something in their baby. When Pharaoh, the leader in Egypt, ordered that all Israelite male babies be destroyed, Moses' parents went to great lengths to see that his life was preserved. I've often wondered what they saw in their newborn that caused them to take such extraordinary steps to see him saved. When our children were born, they were wrinkled and traumatized from the birth process. But Moses' parents saw past that—perhaps they saw a leader and the deliverer of their people.

Moses' parents eventually found a way to comply with Pharaoh's order while preserving the life of their child. They placed their three-month-old son in a basket and floated him down the river. He was found and adopted by Pharaoh's daughter who took and raised him. As her child, Moses received the best education that Egypt could offer.

The price of leadership today is the same as it was for Moses. Education is more important than ever before. In the movie, *Chariots of Fire,* the missions' champion, Eric Liddel, is contrasted with a self-serving runner named Abraham. The latter ran to make himself a name. Eric Liddel ran to glorify God's name.

When Abraham approached a famous coach to ask for his help, the coach responded, "I can't produce miracles. I can't get out of you what God didn't put into you." He was saying that, as a coach, he had to have something to work with to make a world-class runner. And that's the same where leadership is concerned.

Born leaders who are destined to become world-class leaders need to have world-class training. Neither God, nor anyone else for that matter, can get out of you what He or someone else doesn't put in you. If you're going to be a world-class pianist, you need talent, a lot of practice, and good teachers. The more talent you have, the more you need education and training. It's the same with leadership.

In chapter two, I described my governing values, and I hope by now you have developed some of your own. My fifth governing value is, "I am a learner." I need to learn and be educated so that God has something to use and anoint. Remember my premise that leaders are born *and* made. Part of the price of leadership for aspiring leaders is education.

I went back to school at age 37 to earn my doctorate in pastoral ministries (it took me eight years). I have two Masters degrees. I'm certified in four areas of expertise—church growth, meeting planning, time management, and personality profiling. I belong to three professional associations and faithfully read their journals and publications. Last year I read 36 books on such topics as history, theology, leadership, management, and church history.

I subscribe to 10 different magazines and read them all (not cover to cover but I look for articles of interest and keep a clippings file on those areas). I attend at least two conferences every year that will add to my leadership knowledge. I invest in new technology to keep me in touch and to enhance my communication abilities and presentation skills. All these keep me fresh and in tune with what's going on. All these are part of my price of leadership.

While writing this book, I'm reading Nelson Mandela's autobiography, *Long Walk to Freedom.* It's the moving and gripping story of South Africa's leader who helped bring down the apartheid system. Part of his price of leadership was 27 years in jail as a political prisoner. I found it fascinating that Mandela led a campaign in prison to allow inmates the right to study! Many of his fellow political prisoners earned multiple degrees while imprisoned, and Mandela himself worked toward his law degree from a school in England.

When Mandela was released from prison, he was elected the first president of South Africa after apartheid. Why could he serve effectively in that capacity? Because he had paid the price of leadership, and part of that price was education. He stayed relevant and in touch even in an oppressive prison system because he pursued education. How about you?

Now back to Moses. I assume that it was God's will for Moses to attend Egyptian schools. God saved Moses' life and then directed his steps to Pharaoh's house. Education was part of what God had in mind for His future leader. And education may be what God has in mind for you.

I know what you're thinking: "I don't have time." Who does? "I don't have the money." Who does? That's why you need governing values that will help you set priorities that will then determine how you spend your time. You really *do* have the time. You're just spending it on something else right now. And the money will follow when you invest your time properly. As one leader said, "Where it's God's will, it's God's bill."

Do what you can to learn. Read, study, or even enroll in a formal program if possible. Please realize that if you're relying on your gifts and talent only, you're missing out on an important piece of the leadership picture—and not paying the full price of leadership.

So, what are you prepared to do about your education? You're not too old, poor, or unintelligent to get started. Decide what areas of skill and learning would most benefit your leadership position or be most relevant to your area of service. Then find out what options you have. Don't overlook the Internet, which is becoming a major source and means of education.

Once you have made a commitment to get the education and skills that you need, you are ready to embrace the rest of Moses' price of leadership.

Chapter Seven

OUCH!

I was always a good student in school. Most of my grades were A's and B's, and I graduated with honors at every level. When I finished my undergraduate studies, I was accepted to Harvard University's MBA program. Given this academic success, I naively expected that education alone would take me to the highest levels of leadership (and hopefully of financial remuneration!). But I found out that the price of leadership is more than education. It's also acquiring the necessary discipline to complement the education.

Webster's defines discipline as "training that develops self-control, character, or orderliness and efficiency." I've told many leaders that you can buy information, but you can't buy character formation. That takes time, and the path for this discipline is chosen by a higher intelligence—God Himself!

This discipline or training, if properly received, will make you a more effective leader because it teaches you how to follow. It allows you to deal with issues of pride, arrogance, and idealism. It will put you in touch with the realities of life and help you deal with adversity and suffering. The "ouch" will make you more humble and put you in touch with where people are, especially people who are following you. You can't be a good leader until you've learned to be a good follower!

After my graduate studies, I was ready for Wall Street or corporate life, or so I thought. Instead, I found myself working for a chain of trade schools in downtown Pittsburgh. Many nights I came home complaining, "Lord, there must be more for me than this!" But at that time, there wasn't.

I spent four years there learning about myself, and how to deal with some unsavory characters. I learned to serve staff and students who were difficult to deal with, to say the least. Ouch! When I finished there, I went into full-time ministry. Now, I thought, I can get on the leadership track. And I soon found myself an elder and pastor in one of America's leading churches. But that experience was also part of my training, and at times it was painful.

I was part of a pastoral team of 22 men, and I was just about the youngest member. In 11 years on that team, I had many roles of service but no real leadership role. I learned how to be part of a team, how to work (and sometimes suffer) under strong leadership, how to do different jobs that I didn't like or have gifts for, and how to wait. In those 11 years, I spoke in the pulpit twice, and the second time was the last Sunday I was in that church! Ouch!

But all those years were part of my training—discipline and training that are part of every leader's price of leadership. I've never seen it fail. Show me a leader who is successful, and I'll find a similar story—years of preparation in isolation and insignificance. When a leader seems to "suddenly" rise to the top, there usually was a painful period in that leader's life that prepared him or her for that "sudden" rise. There's an "ouch" in every leader's life and history, which prepares the leader as much, if not more so, than any amount of education. That "ouch" brings the necessary discipline and training that complement talent and education.

It was the same for Moses. Let's consider the following excerpt from Stephen's speech in Acts 7 concerning Moses:

> *When Moses was forty years old, he **decided** to visit his fellow Israelites. He **saw** one of them being mistreated by an Egyptian, so he **went** to his defense and **avenged** him by **killing** the Egyptian. Moses **thought** that his own people would realize that God was using him to **rescue** them, but they did not. The next day Moses **came upon** two Israelites who were fighting. He **tried to reconcile** them by **saying**, "Men, you are brothers; why do you want to hurt each other?" But the man who was mistreating the other pushed Moses aside and said, "Who made you ruler and judge over us? Do you want to kill me as you killed the Egyptian yesterday?" When Moses **heard** this, he **fled** to Midian, where he **settled** as a foreigner and had two sons (Acts 7:23-29 emphasis added).*

Moses, armed with the best education in the world, now set out to fulfill his destiny. As mentioned earlier, notice that he knew God was going to use him to rescue the Israelites (he knew his purpose). But also notice all the words that I put in bold in that passage. It's easy to see how full of himself Moses was! He decided, went, avenged, killed, thought, tried, and fled. As the deliverer of Israel, all Moses could do in his raw leadership power was to kill one Egyptian. One down, three million to go!

Once the educational price was paid, Moses needed to be disciplined and trained in order to apply that knowledge. For that, he went on the backside of the desert where he married, raised a family, and tended his father-in-law's sheep for 40 years. When Moses returned to Egypt, he was ready to lead in humility. Instead of using his sword, Moses raised his staff and saw the entire Egyptian army wiped out. Now that's efficient leadership. "Suddenly" Moses appeared on the Egyptian scene, but that was from the Egyptian's point of view. From Moses' point of view, it had been a painful journey to that leadership position.

Many leaders today emulate what I call the Moses' style of leadership. It's the strong, confident leader coming down from the mountain and telling the people what to do on behalf of God, or the board of directors, or the management team. I find that in both the church and business worlds. But these strong leaders don't see the other side to Moses. They don't see that he was developed in isolation over 40 years; that he really didn't want to lead when it was time to lead; that he was a meek and humble leader; and that he diligently served the people he led, to his own detriment. That's what 40 years of training will do to you.

Forty years of training will build character, and character is what makes the most effective leaders. In his book, *The 7 Habits of Highly Effective People,* Stephen Covey points out the shift in modern leadership philosophy from the Character Ethic to the Personality Ethic:

> The Character Ethic taught that there are basic princi-
> ples of effective living [integrity, humility, fidelity,
> temperance, courage, justice, patience, industry, sim-
> plicity, modesty and the Golden Rule], and that people
> can only experience true success and enduring happi-
> ness as they learn and integrate these principles into

their basic character. But shortly after World War I the basic view of success shifted from the Character Ethic to what we might call the Personality Ethic. Success became more a function of personality, of public image, of attitudes and behaviors, skills and techniques that lubricate the processes of human interaction. This Personality Ethic essentially took two paths: one was human and public relations techniques, and the other was positive mental attitude.[12]

Leaders that submit to training tend to follow the Character Ethic; those who don't, seem to be content with the Personality Ethic. Which Ethic will you follow? Will you strive for leadership and get power no matter what you have to do? Will you cover character flaws with personality gimmicks?

There's nothing wrong with knowing that you're a leader. Moses knew that. But that knowledge often comes to help you pay the price of leadership, a price that's often more costly than you first realize.

There is an "ouch" for every leader. There's no telling how long that "ouch" may last or how deep it may go. In fact, the greater your leadership will be, the deeper the "ouch" will go. Don't cut the pain short, but submit to it for the good of your leadership development. And who knows, maybe you'll be like Moses and find yourself one day at the helm of a great organization with many people looking to you for direction and leadership.

The price of leadership for Moses was education in Egypt and then a training program that took him away from Egypt and his ultimate destiny. Those two things together made Moses a leader who changed the world in his day. As we close this section, take some time to assess where you are. Ask yourself the following questions:

Ouch!

1. Am I happy with my level of expertise in my area of work? What can I do to get more education?

2. Am I reading enough and doing all that I can to be on the "cutting edge" of 21st-century information? Are there conferences or programs that I said I would like to attend "one day"?

3. Have I been too eager to lead and not made good use of my current position as part of my training for leadership? Are there areas in my character that need improvement so that I can be a better leader according to the Character Ethic?

The hardest thing for a leader to do is to wait to lead. It's also part of the price of leadership. You may find yourself in a situation that's far away from what you should or will be doing. Don't be too quick to move on, but rather use this time to prepare for what's ahead. For a born leader, however, that can be the hardest part. One leader said that for some, "wait" is a four-letter word!

As I teach and consult on the topic of leadership, people ask me where I got some of the principles I teach. I tell them that I got them from study and from experience. Study without experience is aloof and untested. Experience without study is subjective and unfocused. You need both if you're going to be an effective leader.

Moses was an educated man, and he was a disciplined man. Those two traits made him the leader of millions. Let's look at one other aspect of Moses' price of leadership.

Chapter Eight

HIT IN THE MOUTH BY A BALL

One Saturday morning when my son, John, was 10, he came with me to a softball practice. I had been out of town and wanted to spend some time with him and thought this was a good idea. While we were practicing, the coach asked John to run the bases and simulate some game conditions. He was obviously having fun running and sliding, but I had this fleeting thought: "He's too young to be doing this, and I should ask him to leave the field." I told myself to stop mothering him and allowed him to stay.

Five minutes later a stray throw from the outfield made its way through three players and arrived at second base at the same time my son did. The ball hit him in the mouth and, before I knew it, we were on our way to the hospital where he received eight stitches on the inside of his upper lip. While he was stitching John up, the doctor looked over and saw me turning shades of gray. I think those stitches hurt me more than my son.

As I reflected on that incident, I determined that it contained a leadership lesson. I could have asked my son to leave the field, and he would have obeyed. He may have been mad at me and carried a grudge, or just disappointed. While he was sitting on the sidelines, that ball would have come in from the outfield and rolled to the fence. It would have gone unnoticed, and my son would have never known what my decision saved him from.

Leaders have to be willing to be unpopular for a season. When an organization is in need of leadership because it hasn't had any, those asked to follow can criticize or work against the newly recognized leader. At that point, the leader enters into an entirely new payment plan on the price of leadership. It's painful to lead when people don't want to be led, or when they aren't used to being followers.

That happened to Moses—and he was personally appointed by God Himself! When he arrived back in Egypt, Moses began a series of negotiations with Pharaoh to free the Israelites. Pharaoh responded by taking away the straw provided to the Israelites to make bricks, without lowering their daily quota. The workers quickly reacted in anger—not against Pharaoh, but against Moses, "May the Lord look upon you and judge you! You have made us a stench to Pharaoh and his officials and have put a sword in their hand to kill us" (Exodus 5:21).

This was only the first of many run-ins that Moses had with the people. They consistently challenged his methods and goals. His family criticized his leadership style and his choice of a wife! And Moses often reacted with anger and even rage. In the end, Moses' anger didn't allow him to enter into the Promised Land that he had worked so hard to reach. Instead of speaking to the rock as he was commanded, he misrepresented the Lord and struck the rock in anger.

King Solomon wrote in Ecclesiastes the following words of wisdom: "Do not pay attention to every word people say, or you may hear your servant cursing you—for you know in your heart that many times you yourself have cursed others" (Ecclesiastes 7:22). That is so true! We've all done it at one time or another. So why as leaders are we surprised when people criticize us or don't like us? It hurts because we feel that we're doing our best, and it's just not *fair* to be criticized or unpopular!

One thing I've found that helps me in times like that is a sense of humor. I try to laugh at the situation and myself. We have a saying in our church that if something is going to be funny later, then it's funny now! That makes us work *now* at finding the humor in a difficult set of circumstances. I try to use that strategy especially when leadership tension occurs.

I work hard at humor. I read and save humorous stories and jokes. Once I find them, I try to incorporate them into my leadership opportunities and speaking engagements. I watch comedians (clean ones) and study their style. I've imitated my favorites (Don Rickles, Robin Williams, David Letterman, and Jay Leno) and worked at a style of humor that I can call my own.

I'm convinced that a sense of humor has kept me from "cracking up" at pressure times. It has kept me from taking myself too seriously when people all around me were very serious. And a sense of humor has allowed me to consider that maybe my critics were correct; it has opened me to consider changes that need to be made in my leadership style.

Every great leader in history has been criticized or unpopular. At one time or another, Abraham Lincoln, Franklin Roosevelt, Winston Churchill, Martin Luther King, Nelson Mandela, and a host of others have encountered opposition and even violent attacks. Yet they weathered the storm and were recorded in history as great leaders. Even Jesus was controversial and a topic of conversation by an entire nation! It isn't realistic to think that you won't experience the same challenges as you attempt to lead.

Later we will focus further on King David in Section Four; but for now, I want to close with a story from his early days of leadership. David and his men went out on patrol one day, and when they came back, they found that their city had been ransacked and their wives and children taken captive.

> *When David and his men came to Ziklag, they found it destroyed by fire and their wives and sons and daughters taken captive. So David and his men wept aloud until they had no strength left to weep. David's two wives had been captured—Ahinoam of Jezreel and Abigail, the widow of Nabal of Carmel. David was greatly distressed because the men were talking of stoning him; each one was bitter in spirit because of his sons and daughter* (1 Samuel 30:3-6a).

The men were about to vote David out as their leader. What did David do? The Bible says, "But David found strength in the Lord his God" (1 Samuel 30:6b). Another translation says, "David encouraged himself in the Lord his God" (NAS). Sometimes the price of leadership necessitates that you encourage yourself in what you know to be true and in what you feel your destiny is. When others around you are losing their heads, you must keep yours firmly intact.

There you have it. The price of leadership for Moses was:
- Education
- Discipline and training
- Being misunderstood and unpopular

He paid the price and is today studied and honored as a great leader. How about you? Are you willing to pay the price, and trust that in the end you'll be vindicated and considered a great or courageous leader? I pray that you will so that your leadership will effectively impact your world.

Section Three

VISION, MISSION, AND GOALS FOR THE LEADER

Leaders are people who can create and communicate
visions and strategies because management deals
mostly with the status quo and leadership deals
mostly with change.
—John P. Kotter, *Leading Change*

Chapter Nine

FOLLOW ME!

For a leader to have followers, it's assumed that the leader knows where to go so the leader and followers are on the right track. We've already seen how the leader should also be a servant. How can a leader lead and serve at the same time? How can a leader be out in front and yet accessible and even vulnerable to followers?

The answers to these questions can be confusing for the leader who is used to being in control and out front, or for the leader who wants to be like Moses coming down from on high and delivering the "word of the Lord."

Ken Blanchard helps shed light on these seemingly contradictory questions.

> Leadership is an influence process in which you try to help people accomplish goals. All good leadership starts with a visionary role. This involves not only goal setting but also establishing a clear picture of perfection—what the operation would look like when it was running effectively. In other words, leadership starts with a sense of direction. In the book I coauthored

with John Carlos and Alan Randolph, *Empowerment Takes More Than a Minute,* we said, "A river without banks is a large puddle." The banks permit the river to flow; they give direction to the river. Leadership is all about going somewhere; it's not about wandering around aimlessly. Even Alice in Wonderland learned that concept when she came to a fork in the road and asked the Cheshire cat which road she should take. He replied by asking her, "Where are you going?" She essentially said, "I don't know." His response was quick: "Then it doesn't matter what road you take." If you aren't sure where you are going, your leadership won't really matter, either.[13]

I would add that a river without banks could be in flood stage, and a flood is almost always destructive and dangerous. A movement without boundaries can be like that as well, chewing up people and resources as it changes direction without warning. That's how some leadership styles operate as the creative, spontaneous leader changes the river's course to meet his or her every creative inclination.

Let's return to Max DePree's definition of leadership that we looked at earlier: "The first responsibility of a leader is to define reality." That reality is the direction for the organization, and it has to come clearly from the leadership. The leader or leaders must clearly define the vision and mission for the organization.

I recently met with the chief operating officer for a large Christian ministry. He expressed his frustration with the chief executive officer who was the founder of the organization. The COO said to me, "John, we're in chaos. My leader has changed our vision and mission statement three times *this year*! We are all running around trying to catch up with the changes that he is constantly making!"

Very often leaders (especially if they're the founders of the organization) are the visionaries and in touch with the potential of the organization as they "see" it. That's a critical role. But the day-to-day implementation of that vision belongs to the followers, and the visionary needs to get out of the way and let the followers and staff follow not only the leader, but also the vision and mission of the organization. What a difference that makes!

When a leader sees to it that the followers are following the leader as that leader follows the vision and mission, the leader becomes a servant both of the vision and mission, *and* of the people who are serving the vision! If a leader can keep this picture clear, then followers will be happy and productive, and the vision that the leader first saw has a better chance of becoming reality.

I've been to many seminars on vision, mission statements, and the like, and I've often come away more confused than when I arrived. Some facilitators have made those concepts complicated and rendered them useless for me. And some of the vision and mission statements I've seen have left me less than enthusiastic, or unclear about why the organization exists.

For my own use, I've defined vision, mission, and goals as follows:

- Vision – where you're going
- Mission – how you'll get there
- Goals – when and how you will fulfill your mission

Isn't that simple? It's simple but profound. It's the job of a leader to define the vision and mission so that they are clear to everyone in the organization. The leader can get input on these two concepts, but neither can they be surrendered to a committee, nor do they change according to the creative flow of the leader. When the vision and mission are set, everyone becomes their servant.

I have a small business that I've named the Gold Mine Development Corporation (GMDC). The name came from my first book entitled, *Life Is a Gold Mine: Can You Dig It?* To give you an idea of how my definition for vision and mission can be applied, let me share with you the founding statements of that small organization.

My vision for GMDC is "to help people everywhere find and fulfill their life's purpose." I "see" an army of purposeful people worldwide who are clear about who they are and are not, armed with a simple statement that summarizes their life's purpose. GMDC exists to help them define that purpose. Nothing more, nothing less.

My mission for GMDC is "to conduct seminars, produce publications, and provide other resources that will help people and groups identify their purpose, set goals, and order their lives to accomplish what they were created to be and do." This mission has "led" me to design a website (www.purposequest.com), write books, develop and deliver workshops, and produce a CD-ROM that contains my basic "gold mine" presentation.

I've set goals for how many people I want to reach with live presentations that will help define purpose. In addition, I have a plan for the Africa Gold Mine Development Corporation that specifically identifies, mentors, and equips administrators on that continent. I can do that in my spare time because I'm clear on what my vision is and the mission to achieve that vision.

Let's return to Ken Blanchard to explain further the role of a leader. Earlier in this book I included part of the passage below. I want to include it again for emphasis and to continue with what Blanchard has to say on this subject. He writes,

Most organizations are typically pyramidal in nature. Who is at the top of the organization? The chief executive officer, the chairman, the board of directors. Who is at the bottom? All the employees—the people who do all the work. The people who make the products, sell the products, service the products, and the like. Now there is nothing wrong with having a traditional pyramid for certain tasks or roles. The paradox is that the pyramid needs to be right side up or upside down depending on the task or roles.

It's absolutely essential that the pyramid stay upright when it comes to vision, mission, values, and setting major goals. Moses did not go up on the mountain with a committee. People look to leaders for direction, so the traditional hierarchy isn't bad for this aspect of leadership. While the vision and direction might start with the leader, if you're dealing with experienced people, you want to get them involved in shaping and refining that direction. Some companies, such as W. L. Gore & Associates, do not even have appointed leaders. They think leadership is a follower-driven concept. Therefore, leadership should emerge rather than be appointed. But no matter how the leadership is determined, providing direction is an important aspect of servant-leadership.[14]

A leader "defines reality." How clear is the reality in your organization? If you're a leader, have you clearly spelled out where the organization is going? What's important and what's not? Are you trying to be everything to everyone, or are your core of followers clear on the "soul" of your institution, whether it is a business, church, ministry or non-profit enterprise?

And where are you going? Do you have your hand in every area, whether you have the expertise or not, because it's your "baby" and you can't entrust it to someone else? Be clear on what it is that you bring to the organization's vision and mission and then concentrate on contributing that. Don't try to do it all or be everything, but lead people from your areas of strength. When you do that, you can then work on setting realistic yet challenging goals for the organization and those who work in it.

Chapter Ten

GOALS REVISITED

I've named this chapter "Goals Revisited" because I discussed the issue of goals in my first book, *Life Is a Gold Mine: Can You Dig It?* That discussion focused on setting personal goals, and I stressed that *everyone* can and should set goals for their life. This book, however, is addressed to present and future leaders; so in this chapter, we'll look at organizational goals from a leader's point of view.

John Haggai, founder and president of the Haggai Institute for Leaders in Singapore, writes, "Goal-setting is an ongoing discipline of the true leader. Failure at this point destroys the confidence of the followers because it destroys the credibility of the leader."[15] (I strongly agree.)

It's one thing for a leader to speak about vision and mission, but it's quite another to bring that vision and mission into reality. Without clear goals that make sense to all involved, the vision and mission will never leave the paper on which they are written. And that will undermine the credibility of any leader, no matter how gifted or charismatic.

Haggai continues,

A vision is the foundation of all leadership. The leader's vision requires a commitment to act, which is called a mission. But the vision and mission are put into practice with a set of specific, measurable steps designed to achieve the mission. Those steps are called goals. The vision and mission will remain constant, but the goals should be reviewed monthly or more often. At that review you should assess what goals have been accomplished, examine those that are not completed, determine what corrective measures should be taken, and set new goals.[16]

I've found the issue of goal setting to be where most leaders fail in the leadership process, especially (but not exclusively) those leaders in church or ministry work. This happens for the following reasons:

1. **Relying on the power of the vision** – Many leaders are visionaries who see the end result before it ever exists. They see it so clearly that once they have spoken it, they tend to think that it will take place simply because they have spoken it. A vision needs a mission and a set of goals if it is ever to become a reality.

2. **Changing the vision** – Earlier I mentioned a prominent leader who changed the vision and mission of a major organization three times in one year! Creative leaders tend to live in the creative side of their personality; their own creativity can begin to work against their vision, because visionaries are *always* ready to move on to the next "vision."

3. **Lack of a team approach** – Because leaders usually have the vision, they find it hard to entrust that vision to other people with the experience and skill to bring it to pass.

Consequently, visionaries can micromanage the process, involving themselves in every aspect of the operation and frustrating key, skilled people. This can kill the team approach to accomplishing a vision that is larger than a visionary leader can accomplish.

4. **Haste** – Most leaders are impatient when it comes to taking action. They see the vision and want it delivered *yesterday*. They're in a hurry and don't see the necessity of setting three-, five-, or ten-year goals, not to mention regular accountability meetings to check the progress of the goals.

In my own experience of working with visionary and creative leaders, I've tried to use the annual budget process to focus the organization's goal-setting process. Let me explain.

The budget process at our church, for example, is a mix of business and ministry. We begin our budget process for the upcoming year in September or October. First, I make sure that we are clear about what our income and expenses were in the current year. Then I look at that income and those expenses to determine what to carry over to the next year. I also have to consider if there were special one-time expenses in the current year, or if there were special donations that we can't count on in the coming year.

As part of this process, I then have the staff work on their own evaluations, which are due by the end of the year. I don't evaluate staff; I let them evaluate themselves, and I review what they write. I ask them six questions as part of their evaluation:

1. **Your performance** – Please evaluate your job performance based on your responses that you submitted last December. In what areas were you successful? Where did your performance not measure up to your goals? Why?

2. **Your church/job responsibilities** – What are your basic responsibilities as you understand them? What areas would you like to expand into next year? How can you do your job more effectively? What goals can you set for your area? What can you do to help reduce costs, increase productivity, or increase church membership in the coming year?

3. **Your personal growth** – What steps will you take in the coming year to grow personally or professionally? This should include continuing education, new skills obtained, a book reading program, languages learned, etc. Are there any conferences/training programs that you would like to attend to help you do your job more effectively?

4. **The Great Commission** – What will you do next year to help fulfill the Great Commission to reach all nations with the message of the Gospel? This should include mission trips, volunteer outreach programs here at home, community involvement, and similar efforts.

5. **Your needs from leadership** – Taking all of the above into consideration, what do you need from me and from leadership to do your job and accomplish your goals?

6. **One priority item** – What one *new* project do you think you can start in the coming year that will bring the greatest return to our church? (I will give you an example: for me, it's leadership training.)

Along with this two-page evaluation, I ask each employee to submit a "wish list" for the budget. What is it that they would like to have or do in their area that will cost money and that is consistent with the job goals they're submitting to me?

When we have our estimated expenses, we mix in the

items from the wish list and submit this first draft of the budget to the board of directors. It's at that level that we project what our attendance and income will be for the coming year. From that, we determine what new things from "wish lists" can be included in the budget for approval and what items must stay on the "faith list" pending income from special fundraising projects.

All this serves as the main focal point for our organizational goal-setting. From this, we determine our goals for:

- Annual attendance and growth
- Annual income
- Department-by-department activities
- Individual activities
- New programs and staff

We also determine what projects and activities we won't continue, for every organization needs to honestly and sometimes "ruthlessly" determine what it can't continue in light of current goals and staff.

It's not a sophisticated process, but it works in our setting. (In 1999, we had gross revenues of just under $5 million, a Sunday attendance in excess of 2,000 and a staff of 100 people, not counting the large number of volunteers involved in any number of ministry areas.) The annual budget serves as our collection of goals for the coming year, and we've grown numerically and financially every year since I resumed work with our church. In large part, I would attribute our lack of progress in other areas (such as church planting, missions, and training programs) to our inability to set any specific goals and thus to focus our energies on where we want to go.

Is it time for some honesty in your organization and with your leadership? If your vision and mission are clear, why haven't you been more productive? Could it be a lack of clear goals for whatever reason? I encourage you to sit down with your leadership team and talk about this. Bring in an "outsider" you trust who can help direct your discussions and help you reach some practical conclusions.

Look at every area of your operation and then set practical, achievable goals that are consistent with your vision and mission. And then stick to them until the leadership team decides they are accomplished or need to be abandoned for new goals. Don't settle for strong visionary leadership that's always creative but never productive. Without goals, the vision cannot and will not be achieved. Don't settle for sounding good, but work toward doing good. Your vision is worth the effort.

Chapter Eleven

STOP TO-DO

I try to attend the Peter F. Drucker Foundation annual leadership conference every November. For me, it's always a time to reflect and focus on the coming year. In 1998, Jim Collins, author of *Built to Last,* was on the conference program.

During his presentation, Collins talked of his goal to read 70 books annually. Up to that point in his life, he had read about 35 books in a year's time. Collins told us how he bought a new chair and lamp to facilitate his anticipated increase in reading. At the end of the year, however, he hadn't reached his goal—he still read "only" 35 books.

Collins and his wife tried to determine why they hadn't increased their reading, and they came to the realization that they would have to make some serious adjustments to do so. They got rid of the cable television hookup in their home—and every year after that they consistently reached their goal. "Most of us have a 'to-do' list," Collins said, "but I think as leaders we also need a 'stop to-do' list. We can't keep adding to what we do without at some point taking away something we're already doing to make room for the new activity."

A "stop-to-do" list. What a novel idea! Imagine if you and I and the organizations that we serve began to evaluate our activities with a view toward eliminating those that were outdated. Or stopped doing some things because there were other opportunities that would or could produce greater results. Or had some mechanism that helped us recognize when an activity, even a good activity, no longer served the vision or mission of the organization.

I'm writing this chapter in Morristown, Tennessee, where I'm visiting with a friend and pastor. I've met with his staff several times over the last few months, and we've attempted to restructure and reorganize his operation. The staff has done a wonderful job in responding to the changes, and one staff member told me during her report that she had quit the church music team to take on some new duties.

I wanted to get up and hug her. She had stopped doing something so she could do something else that was more consistent with her job title and duties. Just because she could sing doesn't mean that she needed or was supposed to sing. It's a small thing, I know, but a critical one for leaders to understand.

On the other hand, the organization I work for has had a daily radio broadcast for the last 12 years. We get little response from the listeners (whoever they are), and it generates even less income. Last year, we put strong appeals on the air stating that we needed to hear from the public in order to justify staying on the air. We got six responses! And we're still on the air!

The man who produces the show is ready to move on to something else and is needed in the organization. But radio continues because we don't have any mechanism to evaluate how effective (or ineffective) the radio broadcast is. We're doing it because we've done it for a long time and because every now and then people tell our leadership that they listen. But is it a good investment of time and energy? I argue that it's not, but I regularly lose that friendly argument.

A stop-to-do list. Peter Drucker addresses this issue in several of his publications. I quote here from his book, *Managing in a Time of Great Change*:

> What, then, needs to be done? There is a need for preventive care—that is, for building into the organization systematic monitoring and testing of its theory of the business. There is a need for early diagnosis. Finally, there is a need to rethink a theory that is stagnating and to take effective action in order to change policies and practices, bringing the organization's behavior in line with the new realities of its environment, with a new definition of its mission, and with new core competencies to be developed and acquired.
>
> There are only two preventive measures. But if used consistently, they should keep an organization alert and capable of rapidly changing itself and its theory. The first measure is what I call *abandonment*. Every three years an organization should challenge every product, every service, every policy, every distribution channel with the question, If we were not in it already, would we be going into it now? By questioning accepted policies and routines, the organization forces itself to think about its theory. It forces itself to test assumptions. It forces itself to ask: Why didn't this work, even though it looked so promising when we went into it five years ago? Is it because we made a mistake? Is it because we did the wrong things? Or is it because the right things didn't work?

Without systematic and purposeful abandonment, an organization will be overtaken by events. It will squander its best resources on things it should never have been doing or should no longer do. As a result, it will lack the resources, especially capable people, needed to exploit the opportunities that arise when markets, technologies, and core competencies change. In other words, it will be unable to respond constructively to the opportunities that are created when its theory of the business becomes obsolete.[17]

It's the job of the board of directors or leadership team in any organization to see to it that the limited resources of that entity are directed to activities that are most consistent with the purpose of that entity. Leaders must make sure that the money and people are devoted to the right cause. But often the day-to-day leaders are more in touch with the pulse of the business than the board members and need to help the board understand reality. They need to educate the board members that just because the organization *can* do something doesn't necessarily mean that it *should* do something. It's at that point that leadership has to make the hard decisions, and that, too, constitutes the price of leadership.

At other times, the founder or long-standing leaders have favorite, "pet" projects. They want these projects to continue because they like them, not because they're effective or productive. What's needed is some mechanism to evaluate activities that will clearly identify those that have outlived their usefulness.

Leaders must also do this on a personal basis and learn to say "no." It's hard to say "no," however, if you're not sure what your "yes" is. One of my favorite biblical accounts is found in Acts 6.

In those days when the number of disciples was increasing, the Grecian Jews among them complained against the Hebraic Jews because their widows were being overlooked in the daily distribution of food. So the Twelve gathered all the disciples together and said, "It would not be right for us to neglect the ministry of the word of God in order to wait on tables. Brothers, choose seven men from among you who are known to be full of the Spirit and wisdom. We will turn this responsibility over to them and will give our attention to prayer and the ministry of the word" (Acts 6:1-3).

There are three lessons in this passage that will help you or your organization to stop doing one thing in order to do something new.

1. **Face reality** – As a leader, you must look at reality. Often the phrase "facing reality" is used to refer to the downside of something. But it can also be used for the positive. The apostles faced reality. The early church was growing, and that was good. But growth brought problems, and there was a significant complaint from one of the groups in the church.

Look at all the things that are going well in your life or in your organization. Are you making these things all that they can be? Do you need to pay even more attention to these unexpected success stories? And what about the things that are not going so well? Do you need to keep pouring time and resources into these situations, or is it time to let them go gracefully?

2. **Embrace change** – Letting something go means that there will be change. Up to this point in the life of the early

church, the 12 apostles had been involved in everything. But as the church grew, they could no longer be everything to everyone. They had to delegate and focus on what it was that they did that no one else could do. They didn't personally help the widows, but rather came up with a plan to make sure that the widows were helped.

When I say "embrace" change, I mean just that. While change is necessary for growth and for good leadership, you can't minimize its impact. As a leader, you must be personally involved in helping followers understand the need for the change. Remember how long it took you to get used to the idea of the change. Be patient and give followers the same time to consume and digest the implications of the change. You must also be accessible to develop the plans for change and to help talk out the implications for followers. It's during times of change that followers need to have their closest contact with those in leadership.

3. **Feed your opportunities; starve your problems** – Author Peter Drucker provides us with this phrase, and it's profound. Too often we do the opposite—we feed our problems and starve our opportunities. For instance, I'm not against our radio broadcast per se. I do think it isn't as effective as it once was and has become a problem to produce. As an organization we have many other opportunities before us, and I would like to take the manpower, time, and money we're putting into radio and invest them toward other opportunities. In my mind it's hard to justify putting a lot more time or people toward radio to make it a little more effective. This isn't a "big deal," but a lot of little things can add up to bigger problems.

The apostles in Acts 6 didn't get personally involved in the widow problem; in that sense they "starved" it. Instead, they fed the opportunity to pray and preach the word. The outcome of this strategy was a good one. Acts 6:7 tells us that "...the word of God spread. The number of disciples in Jerusalem increased rapidly, and a large number of priests became obedient to the faith."

Robert Greenleaf also has something to say to leaders about the need to let go of something old in order to embrace the new. He called it "systematic neglect."

> The ability to withdraw and reorient oneself, if only for a moment, presumes that one has learned the art of systematic neglect, to sort out the more important from the less important—and the important from the urgent—and attend to the more important, even though there may be penalties and censure for the neglect of something else. One may govern one's life by the law of the optimum (optimum being that pace and set of choices that give one the best performance over a lifespan)—bearing in mind that there are always emergencies and the optimum includes carrying an unused reserve of energy in all periods of normal demand so that one has the resilience to cope with the emergency.[18]

How about you? What do you need to stop doing in order to undertake a new opportunity? What is no longer yielding the returns that it once did in your life? And how about in the organization you lead? What new opportunities are knocking at the door but can't get in because the "waiting room" is filled with problems? Take out a sheet of paper and make a stop-to-do list, and then have the courage to dialogue with yourself and others about the changes that need to take place.

Chapter Twelve

YEA, TEAM!

Many strong leaders I've worked with (usually the founders of the organizations they lead) don't have a good concept of what a team is or how it functions. Their concept of team is, "I'll tell you what to do and how to do it, and then you can figure out as a team how to get it done. But, oh yes, I have veto power over what you do and the results! And you, not I, will be held accountable for the outcome." When the followers are disgruntled, the leader often points to the bad "team attitude" of the member and can work to isolate or eliminate that member.

As mentioned earlier, a team approach isn't an answer for every problem in an organization. Leaders set the direction for the group and then work to keep things on course. In the case of an emergency or crisis, strong, directive leadership is essential. And not every follower is happy with a team approach. Some want to be told what to do and how to do it to avoid any failure or accountability. And others just want to put in their time for a paycheck.

I've been told that I have some ability to build a team and make if function well. If I have any skill in this area, it's because

I've been part of many "teams" that weren't really teams at all. I was just someone to carry out the wishes of the leader. I try, therefore, to give my fellow team members what I would have liked when I was where they are. These include:

1. **Communication** – When I lead a team, I want open, honest communication. And that takes hard work to achieve for several reasons. First of all, it's hard as a leader to listen and not defend yourself when someone shares something negative about you or your ideas. Second, it's difficult for many followers to speak their mind, since most people have been hurt at some point when they shared their feelings and had them stepped on or ignored. Third, there's a fear among leaders that followers will use information to get more money or to help a competitor at a later date. I recognize the dangers of what I call open communication, but without it, there can't be effective team building. It's that simple.

My office door is almost always open, which tells people that they can come in and talk when they need to. And when they come, I try not to have areas that they can't talk about. For instance, we have many family members on our current church staff. Family-run businesses have strengths and weaknesses, and one weakness is that family issues can spill over into the workplace.

I've had family members come to me about family problems, and I've had non-family members come to me about the family's problems. And I've listened. I've counseled, all the while trying to keep the organization on track, the team functioning, and the people reconciling their differences. I don't sweep these things under the rug or offer pat answers to people that they shouldn't feel that way. If I want a team, then teams communicate real feelings and real problems to successfully accomplish real goals.

I also try to be easy to talk to about money issues. Please don't tell me that this shouldn't affect people and that they just need to "get over it." Money in the workplace affects everyone, and ignoring that is destructive to team building. If someone feels that they've been overlooked or that someone else is making more money and they don't understand why (employees should be able to talk about and know this information), then they should be able to talk to me about this.

For a team to function well, there needs to be a strong degree of trust. Trust is what it takes for communication to flow. Trust must be earned, but it can't be demanded by leaders and earned by followers. I must prove myself trustworthy as a leader and give followers a chance to prove the same. If someone abuses that trust with something I've communicated, I refuse to limit my communication to others. I try to work with the person who abused the trust.

2. **Gratitude** – I wouldn't be where I am today if it wasn't for a whole lot of people who helped me get here. You can talk all you want about giftedness, leadership skills, and the like, but it's people who make any leader effective. And I want to express that gratitude publicly, privately, and profusely. I've found the best ways to do this are:

    a. *Public honor* – Many leaders fear that if they say nice things about someone publicly, that person will ask for more money, or expect more of the same. And they may! If leaders don't say it, however, the team member may also feel used or unappreciated. Everyone likes a pat on the back for a job well done. Doing that publicly doesn't need to lead to problems.

b. *Money* – I've seen the surveys that say people aren't motivated by money or that it isn't one of their basic needs. I say "Baloney!" I don't think most people expect to get it because it doesn't happen very often (and they don't want to appear to be greedy). If you want to express gratitude, give money in the form of a bonus, raise, or gift.

c. *Responsibility* – In professional basketball, a coach and team will help players score on offense if they work hard on defense. Defense isn't glamorous; offense is. Defense is work; offense is fun. I want to show my gratitude for hard work by giving people more freedom and responsibility. I want to "call their number" to score because they've worked hard behind the scenes to help the organization and me.

d. *Training* – I can show gratitude by providing the opportunity and finances for team members to become better at what they do. I'm a big believer in higher education (remember Moses' price of leadership?) and feel that the organization should underwrite the cost whenever possible. That goes for conferences, seminars, books, and technology, as well.

3. **Listening** – You might say that listening should be included under communication, but I've found that it's often not. I've been in "team" meetings where the leader has spoken 90 percent of the time. Real, empathetic listening is perhaps the most important team-building practice there is. People don't expect leaders to do everything they present, but they do expect leaders to listen to what they have to say. When we listen, we're saying that the person we're listening to is a worthy investment of our time, and that what they are saying, even if we disagree, has merit.

It's so hard not to listen with the intent of responding but rather with the intent to understand. I'm constantly training my mind not to prepare a response to the one I'm listening to, and instead to focus on understanding what they're saying. It's even more difficult when that person is sharing something that's critical of me or my decisions.

Steven Covey wrote about listening in his *7 Habits* book referenced earlier. In fact, his fifth habit is "Seek first to understand, then to be understood." I learned from that habit to ask a lot of questions and continually give talkers "feedback" to let them know that I understand what they're saying. I've also learned (and I am still learning) to postpone any response until I've had time to reflect on and digest what was said to me. When I do this, I often come back to the person and say, "I really understand where you're coming from and what you meant when you said that the other day." I may not be in a place to change the situation they addressed, but just listening helps them deal with some reality in their world. It's part of building a team.

Those are my three "secrets" to effective team building: communication, gratitude, and listening. There are more we could discuss under this topic, but those are my top three. If you work on those three, you'll be well on your way to building effective teams no matter what work you're in.

It's time to study another leader and examine the price he paid for his leadership. There's more information about the life of King David in the Bible than anyone else. We follow him from being a shepherd for his father to his dying days as king of Israel. With all that material, we see his successes and failures and the full process of leadership development that he went through. Let's look at his life and leadership now.

Section Four

THE PRICE OF LEADERSHIP
FOR KING DAVID

*He [God] testified concerning him: "I have found
David son of Jesse a man after my own heart;
he will do everything I want him to do"*
(Acts 13:22).

Chapter Thirteen

SERVE TILL YOU DROP

David was a dynamic and charismatic leader. He captured the hearts of people and commanded tremendous loyalty among followers. When King Saul was searching for someone who could come and serve in his court, this is what one of his officials told him about David: "I have seen the son of Jesse of Bethlehem who knows how to play the harp. He is a brave man and a warrior. He speaks well and is a fine-looking man. And the Lord is with him" (1 Samuel 16:18).

David's enemies feared and respected him. He was an organizer, songwriter, musician, warrior, and army captain. While he was born to lead, he learned how to be an effective leader through some difficult times and personal mistakes. Through it all, David never lost sight of his destiny to lead, and his life and leadership are worth studying.

I heard someone say that her life motto was "Shop till you drop." David's motto could have been "Serve till you drop," because early in life, that's just about what he had to do! But service, as mentioned earlier, is good preparation to lead; when you become a leader, your focus changes, but your call to service never does. The first price that David paid for his leadership was learning to serve.

One day when David was a shepherd in his father's house, the king's officials came to him with a job offer. Having heard the good report about David, Saul wanted to hire him to be his personal aide and musician to help him combat depression and an "evil spirit" from God. (Have you ever worked for someone who seemed to have that same problem?) Wow! A promotion! That's pretty heady stuff! David took the job and was good at what he did: "Whenever the spirit from God came upon Saul, David would take his harp and play. Then relief would come to Saul; he would feel better, and the evil spirit would leave him" (1 Samuel 16:23).

This success carried over into other areas of David's job. Shortly after he killed the giant Goliath, people started singing about his military exploits, saying, "Saul has killed his thousands and David his tens of thousands" (1 Samuel 18:7). The public's admiration got David into trouble, for

Saul was very angry; this refrain galled him. "They have credited David with tens of thousands," he thought, "but me with only thousands. What more can he get but the kingdom?" And from that time on Saul kept a jealous eye on David.

The next day an evil spirit from God came forcefully upon Saul. He was prophesying in his house, while David was playing the harp, as he usually did. Saul had a spear in his hand and he hurled it, saying to himself, "I'll pin David to the wall." But David eluded him twice (1 Samuel 18:8-11 emphasis added).

If my supervisor tried to pin me to the wall, I would give him or her a chance to do it only *one* time, and not twice. At that point, I would have felt a strong urge to go somewhere else. But Saul tried to "pin" David to the wall on two occasions, and still David kept playing the harp. When I say that David paid a price to serve, I mean it! He did!

So what happened next? Saul couldn't kill David personally, so he sent him off to war.

Saul was afraid of David, because the Lord was with David but had left Saul. So he sent David away from him and gave him command over a thousand men, and David led the troops in their campaigns. In everything he did he had great success, because the Lord was with him. When Saul saw how successful he was, he was afraid of him. But all Israel and Judah loved David, because he led them in their campaigns (1 Samuel 18:12-15).

I want to make a statement and let you reflect on it for the rest of this section: *David learned more about leadership from Saul than he did from anyone else.* He learned how *not* to lead. Saul used David for his own ends because David was good at what he did. Not only that, but David made Saul feel good and helped him to deal with his problems. Yet Saul went on to torment and harass David for the rest of Saul's life. Yet, for the most part, David continued to serve Israel, Saul, Saul's son Jonathan, and most importantly, the Lord.

After two attempts on his life, we find David back in Saul's presence, fulfilling the musical part of his job description. Saul does it again!

An evil spirit from the Lord came upon Saul as he was sitting in his house with his spear in his hand. While David was playing the harp, Saul tried to pin him to the wall with his spear, but David eluded him as Saul drove the spear into the wall. That night David made good his escape (1 Samuel 19:9).

For a number of years, David fled from Saul's presence, but he still kept his heart of service. How do we know this? Let's consider one more story from David's life that will verify this statement.

When David was told, "Look, the Philistines are fighting against Keilah and are looting the threshing floors," he inquired of the Lord, saying, "Shall I go and attack these Philistines?" The Lord answered him, "Go, attack the Philistines and save Keilah" (1 Samuel 23:1-2).

It was King Saul's job to protect Israel, not David's. But Saul was consumed by his own problems and could not function as king and commander-in-chief. So David, in an attitude of service, did the job that needed to be done. He went and liberated the town of Keilah—and paid a price to do it. When Saul heard where David was and what he was doing, Saul realized that David's service had put him and his troops in a precarious position. Saul immediately moved to take advantage of that position.

Saul was told that David had gone to Keilah, and he said, "God has handed him over to me, for David has imprisoned himself by entering a town with gates and bars." And Saul called up all his forces for battle, to go down to Keilah to besiege David and his men (1 Samuel 23:7-8).

If that wasn't bad enough, the residents of Keilah, who had just been the beneficiaries of David's service, were ready and willing to help King Saul find David!

> *When David learned that Saul was plotting against him, he said to Abiathar the priest, "Bring the ephod." David said, "Oh Lord, God of Israel, . . . Will the citizens of Keilah surrender me to him? Will Saul come down, as your servant has heard? Oh Lord, God of Israel, tell your servant." And the Lord said, "He will." Again David asked, "Will the citizens of Keilah surrender me and my men to Saul?" And the Lord said, "They will"* (1 Samuel 23:9-12).

Those ingrates! David saved them from the Philistines, yet they sided with King Saul who should have saved them in the first place. The Keilahites really knew how to repay a favor.

That's how serving can be sometimes. People may not appreciate what you did or what it cost you to do it. That's why I try to keep a proper focus when I serve—I'm doing it for God and Him alone! Whether anyone sees, notices, or says, "thank you," I'm going to serve and do what I know to be the correct thing no matter the outcome. And believe me, that resolve has been tested over and over again.

I try to keep in mind that my labor is for God, no matter where it takes place and who the recipient is. To help me do this, I've memorized the following verse: "Let nothing move you. Always give yourselves fully to the work of the Lord, because you know that your labor in the Lord is not in vain" (1 Corinthians 15:58). Whether I'm serving a corporation or my church, my labor and service are for Him.

If you remember, one of my governing values is that I am a servant. I can't emphasize enough your need to be a servant-leader. Without an attitude of service, you run the danger of exalting yourself like Saul did and trying to preserve your leadership at any cost. You run the risk of being threatened by others who are more gifted and talented, and allowing that inse-curity to hinder their growth or usefulness to your organization.

It's interesting to consider that David learned more about leadership from Saul than anyone else. David learned how to serve a man who wasn't worthy of David's service. That caused David to learn about authority and to suffer, both of which were part of his price for leadership. Let's look at the issue of authority in the next chapter.

Chapter Fourteen

AUTHORITY

Let's review the soap opera-like life of David that we described in the previous chapter. When we left David, his supervisor (and father-in-law) was trying to kill him. David did a good deed for the villagers of Keilah, and they were ready to betray him. The story continues, and it gets deeper and more serious as far as David is concerned. King Saul, who should be using his army to pursue his enemies, has decided to use it to pursue his servant, David.

> *After Saul returned from pursuing the Philistines, he was told, "David is in the Desert of En Gedi." So Saul took three thousand chosen men from all Israel and set out to look for David and his men near the Crags of the Wild Goats* (1 Samuel 24:1-2).

King Saul just wouldn't give up and was consumed with finding and destroying the man who would be king. But the tables were soon turned, and David was presented a chance to deal with Saul once and for all.

> *He* [Saul] *came to the sheep pens along the way; a*

*cave was there, and Saul went in to relieve himself.
David and his men were far back in the cave. The men
said, "This is the day the Lord spoke of when he said
to you, 'I will give your enemy into your hands for you
to deal with as you wish.'" Then David crept up unnoticed and cut off a corner of Saul's robe* (1 Samuel
24:3-4).

What an opportunity to get Saul off his back. Saul was in a
defenseless position and about as human as you can get. Part
of the price of David's leadership (and yours) was to recognize
the importance of relegating ambition and a self-serving attitude. Even though David knew he was a leader, he had to learn
to respect authority where it already existed. This was vital if
there was going to be any respect for authority when he was
king.

If David rebelled, even in what seemed to be a justifiable
situation, he would have opened the door for others to rebel
against him when he became king. David realized that no
leader is perfect; his own leadership flaws could open the door
for a takeover when he became king. He chose not to set that
example, and he let Saul "off the hook."

*Afterward, David was conscience-stricken for having
cut off a corner of his robe. He said to his men, "The
Lord forbid that I should do such a thing to my master,
the Lord's anointed or lift my hand against him; for he
is the anointed of the Lord." With these words David
rebuked his men and did not allow them to attack Saul.
And Saul left the cave and went his way* (1 Samuel
24:5-7).

David refused to take part in this "hostile takeover." He decided not to become a leader by deposing the leader that was in

his place. Notice that David called Saul "the anointed of the Lord." Saul wasn't a priest or holy man; he was the king. David realized that Saul was in that position because God put him there. David wasn't going to take matters into his own hands and make himself king. Instead, David respected the authority that Saul had even though Saul had abused it.

If it's "in" you to lead, then that's what you want to do. When an opportunity presents itself to lead and you're a leader, everything in you wants to assume the role. It makes sense and seems to be what needs to take place. It's at that point that you have to ask yourself what price you're willing to pay for that leadership. Is part of the price for establishing your position the pain or embarrassment of the previous leader who was ousted, even for good reason? It may be, but if it is, make sure that you didn't play a role in the ouster. Respect the office if you can't respect the officer, and remember that the same people who are putting you in "took out" your predecessor. They can do it to you.

David spared Saul one more time after the incident just described. Saul was sleeping in a field when David came up unnoticed. David once again confronted Saul with evidence to show that David could have killed him but chose not to do so. Saul wept in sadness when confronted with his own ruthlessness, but didn't really change. Finally, Saul was killed in battle and his son, Ish-bosheth, replaced him as king while David became the king over his own tribe of Judah.

When Saul died at the hand of his Philistine enemies, an ambitious young man set out to inform David of the situation. Along the way he decided to change the story of how it happened in hopes of securing a favored position with David. When he arrived to tell David, this is what transpired:

Then David said to the young man who brought him the report, "How do you know that Saul and his son Jonathan are dead?" "I happened to be on Mount Gilboa," the young man said, "and there was Saul, leaning on his spear, with the chariots and riders almost upon him. When he turned around and saw me, he called out to me, and I said, 'What can I do?' . . . Then he said to me, 'Stand over me and kill me! I am in the throes of death, but I'm still alive. So I stood over him and killed him . . ." (2 Samuel 1:5-10).

This young man didn't actually kill Saul, but he wanted David to think that he did. What was David's response? He killed the young man, saying, "Why were you not afraid to lift your hand to destroy the Lord's anointed?" David knew that if that were indeed true, the young man would not hesitate to do the same to David one day. But more importantly, the young man didn't respect authority.

David ruled in Judah seven more years while Ish-bosheth's rule grew weaker and weaker. Finally, someone stepped forward to take action.

Now Recab and Baanah, the sons of Rimmon the Beerothite, set out for the house of Ish-bosheth, and they arrived there in the heat of the day while he was taking his noonday rest. They went into the inner part of the house as if to get some wheat, and they stabbed him in the stomach. . . . They had gone into the house while he was lying on the bed in his bedroom. After they stabbed and killed him, they cut off his head. Taking it with them, they traveled all night by way of the Arabah. They brought the head of Ish-bosheth to David at Hebron and said to the king, "Here is the head of Ish-bosheth son of Saul, your enemy, who tried to take your life. This day the Lord has avenged my lord the king against Saul and his offspring" (2 Samuel 4:5-8).

Maybe these two men truly felt they had to take matters into their own hands and kill the existing king so that David could take over. I suspect that they hoped to "get in good" with David by killing the one whom they thought stood between him and the top position. But David wasn't impressed with their actions.

David answered Recab and his brother Baanah, the sons of Rimmon the Beerothite, "As surely as the Lord lives, who has delivered me out of all trouble, when a man came and told me, 'Saul is dead' and thought he was bringing me good news, I seized him and put him to death in Ziklag. That was the reward I gave him for his news! How much more—when wicked men have killed an innocent man in his own house and on his own bed—should I not now demand his blood from your hand and rid the earth of you!" So David gave an order to his men, and they killed them. They cut off their hands and feet and hung the bodies by the pool in Hebron. But they took the head of Ish-bosheth and buried it in Abner's tomb at Hebron (2 Samuel 4:9-12).

I remember a time in my career when I was approached by another firm and had preliminary discussions for a new job with a much higher salary. I had two initial interviews and I was asked what needed to happen next. My request was unusual: I asked the company to call my current supervisor to ask permission for the talks to proceed. I didn't want to be negotiating behind my boss's back, and I wanted to be on as good terms as possible if I did indeed leave. The owner of the company who was interviewing me refused to do that, and the negotiations broke down. I didn't get that new job (along with a significant raise) because, in this case, I wanted to respect the one in authority on my existing job.

On another occasion, I was asked to come in and take over the director's position for a non-profit organization. That was awkward because I was being asked to replace the person who had gotten me involved as a consultant and trainer in that organization! I kept my distance until the director was relieved of his duties. When I took over the helm of the organization, I then reached out to my predecessor and included him on all future team events.

At our first staff meeting, I recognized him for all his hard work and made a public commitment to him and the team he had built to be his friend. When I stood in his wedding two years later, I knew that I had treated him and his position with respect, for we were still friends even though I had replaced him as director.

Ultimately, I was working to keep my ambition under control and to honor the leadership that had worked to bring the organization to the place where it could hire me. I think that's the price of leadership for anyone—to respect the authority that he or she hopes to have one day. I can't control anyone else's ambition, but I have to control my own. One of the ways I've tried to do this is by honoring those in authority, even if they didn't deserve the honor.

I would be less than honest if I didn't tell you that this principle of honoring authority can be very costly, for it introduces a level of suffering that works deep inside you. The account shows that David suffered greatly at the hands of Saul. But that suffering prepared David to be the finest king the world has ever known. Suffering is the final price David had to pay for his leadership, and it may be a price you have to pay for yours. As we close this section on David, let's consider this issue of suffering.

Chapter Fifteen

NO PAIN, NO GAIN

Who coined the phrase used as this chapter's title? I have no idea, but it's a cute rhyme that is so very accurate—especially where leadership is concerned. When we looked at Moses, we touched on the issue of suffering as part of the price for leadership. Moses spent 40 years on the far side of the desert tending his father's sheep. That discipline or training must have been a lonely, frustrating time. Having seen the finest that Egypt had to offer, Moses spent the mid-years of his life seeing the barrenness of the desert and talking to sheep that couldn't talk back. That had to be painful. If "no pain, no gain" is true, then he gained a lot during those 40 years.

Then there was pain and suffering when Moses became Israel's leader. There was the pain of confusion, rejection, hard work, and facing his shortcomings. The people he led repeatedly complained about the conditions and the leader. Leading millions of people through a desert land for 40 years was no walk in the park! If "no pain, no gain" is true, Moses' 40-year stint as leader must have gained him a lot!

Now we come to David, and the pain and gain were no less

real in his life—no less part of his price of leadership. Why does suffering play such a large part in leadership training and the actual job of leading? There are several reasons.

1. **Leadership is a skill carried out by imperfect people in an imperfect world.** Leaders aren't perfect; neither are followers. Both tend to make mistakes in judgment, and some of those mistakes can lead to bankruptcy and even loss of life. Most leaders face crises getting to positions of leadership and also after they are in leadership. Many of these crises are brought on by mistakes and some by events beyond anyone's control—they are considered by the insurance industry as "acts of God."

2. **Leaders care.** People usually don't pay the price to lead unless they care passionately about something—the cause they're leading, money, success, power, or the people they're serving. When things don't go as they ought to, leaders can stay up nights, get ulcers, ruin their health, or age prematurely.

3. **Leaders are vulnerable.** Because of their position out front, leaders seldom lead in a vacuum. People watch and evaluate what they do. Imagine that you're the CEO of a publicly-held corporation that's losing money and market position. Chances are you'll be fired—publicly! Your "sins" will be paraded before the business community, and you'll be exiled to unemployment, hopefully with a large severance pay (well, maybe it's not all suffering!).

4. **Leaders grow.** Effective leaders never stop growing. They're eager—or at least willing—to learn new techniques, methods, and knowledge. More importantly, leaders grow as human beings, and suffering opens a

leader to new levels of self-understanding that can't be learned in any school.

David suffered in his life and leadership. You can't read the psalms he wrote without feeling the pain he went through to get the gain. Enemies pursued him, family and friends betrayed him, his followers criticized him, and his own failures brought hardship to him and those he served and loved.

David had to wait 25 years between the time he was identified as the next king and when he actually took the throne. When he did become king, his sons fought over the right to be his successor. All these things made David the leader that we've come to know. It wasn't just his tremendous giftedness and skill; it was how he related to suffering and what he learned from it that set David—and that will set you—apart from ordinary leaders.

As I reflect on my 50 years of life, I've learned more through the tough, painful times than through the good times. When I was downsized out of a position I loved in 1995 and had to relocate back to my hometown, I suffered. I was humiliated that my department had to be phased out because we were out of money. I felt that people blamed me for the situation.

My family wasn't anxious to move again, and we had to suffer through that transition. I really didn't want to go back into local church work, but had little choice since that was the door that seemed to open to me. There are many aspects of that world that I enjoy, but there are other parts that bring me pain and suffering.

My pain and suffering have brought me a lot of gain. I'm, however, not the same leader I used to be. I'm still intense, but less so with other people and their feelings. I've learned to be more patient with myself and others, especially when things don't go right. I can truly empathize with *anyone* who has lost a job or had their leadership skills questioned, because I've been there.

When you suffer, you know what someone else is going through firsthand. Armed with that knowledge, you can talk to them heart-to-heart and provide real relief.

There are pain and gain that come from serving as well. There is the pain of not being recognized for work done, of seeing others get credit for the work you did. When you serve well, seldom does anyone know the time, effort, or pain that went into your effort. You can work hours on a project that can be over in a matter of minutes.

There's no question that my leadership is more complete, more "human" today because of what I have suffered and am suffering. I take comfort that I'm not alone. When I suffer as a leader, I join with my fellow leaders through the ages who have suffered and endured pain to make their world a better place for others.

As we close this section, I want to look at the issue of suffering in the life of Jesus. It's documented in all four Gospel accounts that Jesus suffered, not only in death but in His life and ministry. He was criticized, betrayed, debated, and questioned. Things didn't always go well for Him, but He provided a legacy of how to behave while suffering that His followers have embraced for centuries. There is one passage in particular that speaks to His role as "suffering prophet."

Because he [Jesus] *himself suffered when he was tempted, he is able to help those who are being tempted. . . . Although he was a son, he learned obedience from what he suffered and once made perfect, he became the source of eternal salvation for all who obey him and was designated by God to be high priest in the order of Melchizedek* (Hebrews 2:18; 5:8-10).

From these verses, we see that suffering prepares a leader to

1. **Identify and help others who are encountering what the leader has gone through** – Because Jesus suffered, He understood that process firsthand and could provide real and not theoretical help to others.

2. **Not rely on relationship alone as the basis for leadership** – He led not because He was a Son, but also because He paid the price.

3. **Be promoted** – When people see you and how you handle real life, they're better able to entrust even greater authority and power to you.

4. **Be a source of wisdom and help** – When people know you know what you're talking about and are willing to help them, they will come to you for advice, mentoring, and career help.

To review, David's price of leadership was

1. **Service** – He served King Saul, his predecessor, with loyalty and faithfulness in the midst of personal danger and confusion.

2. **Authority** – He learned to respect the office and authority even if he couldn't respect the officer and the one who had the authority. He refused to base his leadership on a rebellion against the powers-that-be.

3. **Suffering** – David had to wait to gain the throne and, during that waiting period, suffered many things. His suffering, however, prepared him to be a gracious and magnanimous king and a leader worth studying and emulating.

I hope that you will indeed study and apply David's leadership style where and when you can. I once again point you to Robert Greenleaf's material on servant-leadership. Also study the lives of other leaders in history and discover the suffering they went through to get to the top. See how they handled themselves in crises and learn from their mistakes and successes. All this will help you to be the leader that God wants you to be and one whom people will follow.

Section Five

MANAGING YOURSELF AND YOUR TIME

More and more people in the workforce
—and most knowledge workers—
will have to MANAGE THEMSELVES.
They will have to place themselves
where they can make the greatest contribution;
they will have to learn to develop themselves.
They will have to learn to stay young and mentally alive
during a fifty-year working life.
They will have to learn how and when to change what
they do, how they do it and when they do it.
—Peter F. Drucker,
Management Challenges for the 21st Century

Chapter Sixteen

YOU'VE GOT ALL
THE TIME IN THE WORLD

Time is the great equalizer among people and leaders. You may not have as much talent, skill, or money as someone else. For every day you're alive, however, you have as much time—24 hours a day—as anyone else. What you do with that time will determine how successful you are and how effective your leadership will be.

When you think of it, you really *do* have all the time in the world. What are you doing with it? I've found that effective time management is a key element in the successful style and role of any leader. A leader must learn to manage those 24 hours—to avoid the tyranny of the urgent and focus on what is truly important and the highest priority out of all the available priorities.

Peter Drucker, when discussing the issue of leadership focus, tells an interesting story about the composer Mozart:

Very few people know where they belong, what kind of temperament and person they are. "Do I work with people, or am I a loner?" And "What are my values?

What am I committed to?" And "Where do I belong? What is my contribution?"

And this is, as I said, unprecedented. Those questions were never asked—well, yes, the super achievers asked them. Leonardo DaVinci had one whole notebook in which he asked these questions of himself. And Mozart knew it and knew it very well. He's the only man in the history of music who was equally good on two totally different instruments. He wasn't only a great piano virtuoso; he was an incredible violin virtuoso. And yet, he decided you can only be good in one instrument, because to be good, you have to practice three hours a day. There are not enough hours a day, and so he gave up the violin. He knew it, and he wrote it down. We have his notebooks.

The super achievers always knew when to say "No." And they always knew what to reach for. And they always knew where to place themselves. That makes them super achievers. And now all of us will have to learn that. It's not very difficult. The key to it—what Leonardo did and Mozart did—is to write it down and then check it.[19]

Can you imagine being equally world-class in two things and quitting one of them? That really is unprecedented. Mozart, however, still impacts the world with his music because he realized that he had all the time in the world—but not all the time there was. He realized that he was finite and had to make choices about what to do with his time, with those 24 hours a day available to each and every leader. With that in mind, he quit one instrument to concentrate on the other.

Notice that Drucker spoke of values, knowing what's important to you. Those values should guide your decisions on what to do and what not to do. Then you need to write those down and check your progress and focus from time to time. (If you skipped developing your values as discussed in chapter two, go back now and make up the assignment you missed. This is critically important.)

When I speak about time management to groups of leaders, I usually share my six time-management friends—principles and skills that have made me more effective in the management of my time. I talked about four of these friends in my book, *Life is a Gold Mine: Can You Dig It?* Since then, I've added two more. This book isn't about time management, but these concepts are vital to this section on self-management.

1. **The book of Proverbs**. I love the book of Proverbs in the Old Testament. I've studied it for 25 years, and I still find things in it I've never seen before. What I like best is how practical it is. It contains much useful information on how to live life and how to lead. To my surprise, it also contains material on how to manage time.

To effectively manage your time, you need wisdom. We'll define and study wisdom in the next section when we look at the life of the Old Testament leader Daniel. But for now, let me just mention that wisdom enables you to creatively do things that you've never done before. That's important in time management because every day is different and presents new opportunities and challenges. As you enter new seasons of your life, you need wisdom to navigate the challenges of staying on course and remaining focused.

The daily readings in my book, *A Daily Dose of Proverbs,* contain many insights on effective time management. I encourage you to use them as a daily guide to help you prioritize your world. For the sake of this discussion, let me quote one verse that has become my "friend" as I manage my time: "For by me [wisdom] your days will be multiplied, and years of life will be added to you" (Proverbs 9:11 NAS).

From that verse, I see that I can effectively "multiply" my days and consequently my effectiveness by applying wisdom where time is concerned. Since Proverbs is a source of wisdom, it's my first friend where time management is concerned.

2. **A time management system**. I use the classic size, Monticello-style Franklin Covey time management system as my notebook to write things such as those that Drucker recommended. It has two pages for every day of the year, and it gives me room to include my prioritized daily task list (something I do almost every day), notes from daily meetings, meeting agendas, and discussion lists for each of my key staff people that include projects they are working on.

A yellow tablet and spiral notebook aren't systems. They're places to write things down, but there's little or no chance of retrieving what you record in one of them. I want and need a place to record not only my daily tasks, but my values, job description, goals, long-range projects, key ideas, quotes for review, and my calendar. The planner system I use provides all that and more, and I carry it with me wherever I go. When someone sees me write something to do in my planner, they know it's as good as done because I'm committed to use that system to keep me focused and on track.

3. **My computer**. I have a laptop computer, and it gets a lot of use as well. It saves me time and effort as I travel. It allows me to access my e-mail anywhere in the world (I usually check my messages 4-5 times a day, and I have a reputation for a quick response to e-mail messages sent to

me) and it is also my writing companion for this book. I don't have the slightest idea how a computer works or what many of the terms mean. I just know that the computer is my friend when it comes to efficiency, leadership, and time management.

I'm surprised how many leaders don't have or use a computer, or who underutilize it in their leadership role. There's no excuse for not having a computer and no excuse for not effectively using it. If I can use one, anyone can and should. You can't be serious about time management without one.

4. **When in doubt, throw it out!** A time management expert advised me one time not to go through work to get to work. I listened to what she told me, and I am ruthless when it comes to paperwork. At least twice a year, I "clean out" my office and home files, books, and articles. I refuse to keep anything that I can easily retrieve through some other source. I do the same thing with my computer and regularly work to dump files that I haven't used in the previous 12 months.

I don't like to look at stacks of "stuff" that accumulate because I may need them one day. I especially don't like wading through piles to find what I need. So I have an adequate filing system and throw out lots of papers and letters. If there's any doubt, then I usually throw it out and have seldom had any regrets. This "friend" has saved me a lot of time and trouble, and kept my busy world streamlined and efficient.

5. **Delegation**. This friend is closely related to the team-building principle that we discussed earlier. I've found that if I build a team, I have more people around me who may enjoy doing something that I dread or just tolerate.

Delegation also rewards people for hard work by giving them more responsibility and challenge in the workplace.

Alec MacKenzie, time management author and expert, wrote, "The two key points to keep in mind about delegation: Do it (so you don't spend time doing things others could or should be doing) and do it right (so you won't have to spend time undoing a poor job)."[20] Delegation isn't abandoning tasks and people but rather working with the team to help them be successful and grow in their abilities and responsibilities. Delegation is my friend because it allows me to expand my leadership without dominating the followers. You should know how important this concept is at this point in our study.

6. **Written goals**. I like to write out my goals for the coming year and have done so for a number of years. Merrill and Donna Douglass said it best when they wrote:

   Many of us think that writing goals is unnecessary. We often say that we keep goals in our head, and as long as we think about them it doesn't matter whether or not the goals are written down. This is dangerous reasoning. The purpose of writing goals is to clarify them. There seems to be a special kind of magic in writing goals. Once a goal is written, you have more invested in it than before.[21]

My goals come from my values and tell me what is important. My goals keep me (most of the time) from investing time in matters that don't matter. For instance, I want to write a book every year for the next 10 years. I have five of the titles and topics chosen. That goal will keep me focused when I travel and when I'm home, and when other things clamor for my attention and time.

These six friends keep me from wasting all the time in my world:

- The book of Proverbs
- A time management system
- My computer
- When in doubt, throw it out!
- Delegation
- Written goals

How many of these friends are in your life? Are there other friends that aren't included that have helped you use your time more effectively? I hope there are, because my desire would be for you to manage your time well as a leader or leader-in-training. You and I need all the help we can get. With that in mind, let's move on to look at more of what Peter Drucker has to say about managing oneself.

Chapter Seventeen

KNOW THY TIME

Almost every year out of the last 15, I have read Peter Drucker's book, *The Effective Executive.* It challenges me every time I read it, and I learn something from every reading. The chapter titles tell you something about why I like this book:

- Effectiveness Can Be Learned
- Know Thy Time
- What Can I Contribute?
- Making Strength Productive
- First Things First
- The Elements of Decision-Making
- Effective Decisions
- Effectiveness Must Be Learned

This book was written in 1966 but is as relevant today (perhaps more so) as when it was first published. Of particular interest to our study of leadership is the chapter, "Know Thy Time." Since that has had such an impact on me, and since imitation is the highest form of flattery, I've chosen that title for this chapter.

In that particular chapter, Drucker introduced an idea and exercise that I use regularly: the time inventory. I discuss it in *Life Is a Gold Mine* and I include a quick overview here.

Drucker advocates (and so do I) an annual analysis of where your time goes. As a leader, your time and how you spend it is critical, so a time inventory can help you make adjustments and decisions to make your leadership more effective.

> That one has to record time before one can know where it goes and before, in turn, one can attempt to manage it we have realized for the best part of the century. . . . But we have not applied it to the work that matters increasingly, and that particularly has to cope with time: the work of the knowledge worker and of the executive. . . . The first step toward executive effectiveness is therefore to record actual time.[22]

Drucker advocates that this be done at a minimum for a three- or four-week stretch twice a year. I haven't found it practical to do it that often, so I have settled on once a year for a two-week period. If you can do more, great. If not, at least try to do what I do.

I keep a record in my planner of what I do in half-hour sections of the day. I identify whether it is planning, telephone, personal meetings (with whom and toward what purpose), writing, or projects (again recording what project and for what purpose). I do my best to log interruptions and how long they lasted.

After a two-week period, I then take the total number of hours I logged and begin to break down the individual time spent on the various categories mentioned above. I calculate the percentage of the time that I spent on the telephone, in personal meetings, in private work, and on certain projects. I also total my interruptions and what percent they were of my total time.

Another thing I log is time spent in reading and watching television. At one point in my life, I was conducting time management training sessions on a regular basis. I took great pride in telling the participants that I didn't watch that much television. After my time log, I discovered that wasn't true. I had watched 14 hours per week during the two weeks I analyzed!

That provides another reason to do an inventory. You don't always know or realize where your time is going, and you can be easily misled. When I saw the amount of time used for television that I could have used for reading, rest, or family time, I made some definite changes in my behavior. The time log or inventory helped me do it.

In an earlier chapter, I told the story of Jim Collins who didn't reach his book-reading goal until he got rid of cable television. He found that he had the time to read; he was simply using that time on another activity. Your time inventory can help you reclaim time that is going toward some unproductive activity.

You'll discover more than time wasters from your log. You'll also be able to see how much time you're spending on worthwhile projects that perhaps can be given to someone else or streamlined. One such area would be meetings. How many hours are you now spending in meetings? What would happen if you shortened every meeting by 30 minutes? How much time would that give you each day?

It doesn't seem possible to do that until you look at how much time is spent in meetings socializing, not starting on time, and how much time is wasted without an agenda. Or perhaps you spend a lot of time on the phone. Maybe e-mail or a written fax would cut out the wasted time in conversation and free up more time for something else. There is no end to the creative ways you can use your time log and inventory. But to use one, you have to do one.

All these benefits to keeping a log are helpful, but the greatest task is to reclaim and group what Drucker calls "discretionary" time. He defines this as time that is "available for the big tasks that will really make a contribution."[23] Drucker makes an effective case, borne out by your own experience, that "the higher up the executive [leader], the larger will be the proportion of time that isn't under his control and yet not spent on contribution. The larger the organization, the more time will be needed just to keep the organization together and running, rather than to make it function and produce."[24] The better the leader, the greater the demands that are placed by the organization on his or her time. This requires proactive steps if the leader is to be a leader in more than name and reputation.

Drucker continues:

> The effective executive [leader] therefore knows that he has to consolidate his discretionary time. He knows that he needs large chunks of time and that small driblets are no time at all. Even one quarter of the working day, if consolidated in large time units, is usually enough to get the important things done. The final step in time management is therefore to consolidate the time that record and analysis show as normally available and under the executive's [leader's] control.[25]

As I work to finish this book, I've had to stop writing in half-hour blocks of time and "clear the decks" to do some serious writing. It's also the time of year for taxes, so I must include that activity as well. Today I'm devoting six hours to writing and three to tax preparation. I've claimed some discretionary time. But I can't do that tomorrow, because the operation of my business needs me and so do the people I work with. A leader's time isn't always his or her own, as you are only too aware.

Are you managing your time well? In the midst of demands to meet, serve, solve problems, and maintain, are you finding and claiming time to do the things that will keep your leadership sharp, growing, and effective? Consider doing the following things to help block out chunks of leadership time:

1. Work at home one day a week.

2. Work at home in the mornings or afternoons on a regular basis.

3. Go to your calendar and put an "x" through one day every month that will serve as a retreat day. Then go off to some hotel or hideaway to work on something without interruption.

4. Think of some other way or technique that will give you time to be the leader you need to be today.

As we close this chapter, consider these final words from Drucker's book, *The Effective Executive:*

> Time is the scarcest resource, and unless it is managed, nothing else can be managed. The analysis of one's time, moreover, is the one easily accessible and yet systematic way to analyze one's work and to think through what really matters. "Know Thyself," the oldest prescription for wisdom, is almost impossibly difficult for mortal men. But everyone can follow the injunction "Know Thy Time" if he [or she] wants to, and be well on the road toward contribution and effectiveness.[26]

As we close this chapter on "Know Thy Time," let's now take a look at that adage Drucker mentioned, "Know Thyself." It does play an important part in managing oneself and can make all the difference in your own leadership role.

Chapter Eighteen

KNOW THYSELF

When I was growing up, I would tell people that I wanted to be a priest. I don't know why. There was something attractive about the job, and it seemed like you had an inside track on serving God, something I felt called to do.

After graduate school, while working as a financial aid officer for a chain of trade schools, I began to prepare for the ministry. My pastor began to mentor me and expose me to the things I would need to be a successful pastor. I eventually enrolled in a seminary and received a masters and doctorate in pastoral ministries. In 1989, I became the pastor of a church in Orlando, Florida, and pastored that church for four years.

There was only one problem. I found out that I didn't like pastoring. More than that, I discovered that pastoring didn't like me! I was a task-oriented individual functioning in a career and position that required a lot of people-oriented skills. While those skills could be (and were) learned, they still took a lot of energy and generated a lot of stress. I wasn't a happy leader because I wasn't leading where I could utilize my strengths to the fullest.

There was one tool that helped me come to this realization.

At the urging of a friend, I completed a profile called "The Personality System" published by The Institute for Motivational Living, Inc., in New Castle, Pennsylvania. This profile is also known by the acronym DISC profile, because it identifies four behavioral styles that begin with the letters DISC.

First of all, my profile results showed that I was under tremendous stress and pressure trying to be all styles to all people. That's what the ministry can do to someone who feels the pressure to adapt to everyone's expectations, something I was trying to do to be a "good" pastor. The profile went on to show that I was a "C" style (which stands for compliant, correct, and conscientious) with a "D" style to back that up (the "D" is short for driving, determined, and dominant). I was a task-oriented individual who liked projects and tasks and the challenges that came with them.

The profile indicated that I was very low in the "I" style (which stands for influencer, a very verbal, relational style) and also low in the "S" style (which stands for steady, secure and one that likes routine and the status quo). In short, I functioned best in a situation that required strong administrative and organizational skills, and less so in a situation that required a lot of interpersonal contact and nurture. I wasn't cut out to be a pastor.

Armed with that information, I eventually resigned the pastorate to take a job with Integrity Music as director of their conference and educational division. That began three of the happiest and most fulfilling years of my life. Now that I'm back in church work, I'm more knowledgeable of who I am and who I'm not. Now I do pastoral things, but I avoid being drawn into all the activities of the pastorate and maintain a good percentage of my time in the areas of administration, project management, and team building.

That DISC profile caused me to look at who I was and wasn't. It's not a magic profile nor is it perfect or psychologically sophisticated. (If you would like to take this profile, you can contact my office through the phone numbers and e-mail address provided at the end of this book.) It was enough to get me started on a path of self-understanding that has enhanced my leadership abilities. I stopped trying to be what I wasn't and began to strengthen and improve what I was. That has made me a better and more effective leader.

Peter Drucker's latest book, *Management Challenges for the 21st Century,* addresses this very issue of self-knowledge. Drucker encourages leaders to develop a feedback analysis. This is done "whenever one makes a key decision, and whenever one does a key action, one writes down what one expects will happen. And nine or twelve months later one then feeds back from results or expectations."[27]

From this, Drucker summarizes three action conclusions from the feedback analysis:

1. **Concentrate on your strengths.** Place yourself where your strengths can produce performance and results.

2. **Work on improving your strengths.** The feedback analysis rapidly shows where a person needs to improve skills or has to acquire new knowledge. It will show where skills and knowledge are no longer adequate and have to be updated. It will also pinpoint gaps in your knowledge.

3. **Work to correct disabling ignorance.** This he describes as areas of weakness that undermine one's strengths.[28]

My profile not only helped me to identify my strengths but also to work on my own disabling ignorance. While my profile showed my task orientation, it also revealed how little I understood people who weren't like me or where they were "coming from." I realized how rough I could be working with people who were motivated by relationship and routine—that represented my disabling ignorance.

I began to work on understanding what motivated people unlike me and began to apply what I learned. I was still motivated by my strength of getting the job done, but I was complementing that strength by learning how to motivate people and win their support. In this way I made my strengths of project management fully productive.

I've had to improve my people skills if I was going to be fully productive because the projects I oversee all involve people. To not improve in this area would be to render my strengths useless or less than they could be, and that wasn't acceptable to me.

In knowing myself, I've come to some other conclusions about who I am and am not. I've discovered that:

1. I love to travel, partly because of the challenge it presents that satisfies my "D" style and partly because it gives me uninterrupted chunks of time to read, write, and work on projects that require uninterrupted time.

2. I can work with people, but when I do, I need to schedule some "down time" somewhere after that to replenish and recharge my "batteries."

3. I am a morning person, working best in the early hours on writing and projects. I need to leave busy work, phone calls, meetings, and follow-up for the afternoon.

4. I enjoy working for a big organization where there are lots of activities and opportunities.

5. I'm a city person. I like traffic, people, and congestion. The mountains or nature hold no special blessing for me. I work best when I'm in a city environment.

6. I prefer to listen as a way to learn, but I don't mind reading. For me, it's not either/or.

I've included those few personal likes and dislikes to show that I've worked on understanding who I am. I'm still learning, but I've taken seriously Drucker's challenge to self-knowledge:

We will have to learn where we belong, what our strengths are, what we have to learn so that we get the full benefit from it, where our defects are, what we are not good at, where we belong, what our values are. For the first time in human history, we will have to learn to take responsibility for managing ourselves. And as I said, this is probably a much bigger change than any technology—a change in the human condition. Nobody teaches it—no school, no college—and [it] probably will be another hundred years before they teach it.

In the meantime, the achievers—and I don't mean the millionaires, but rather the ones who want to make a contribution, who want to lead a fulfilling life, and want to feel that there is some purpose in their being on this earth—will have to learn something which, only a few years ago, a very few super achievers ever knew. They will have to learn to manage themselves, to build on their strengths, to build on their values.[29]

That's what leaders will have to do more and more in the coming years. If you're going to be effective and have people follow you, you must know yourself and not try to be everything to everyone. You will also have to release followers from the same pitfall. If you insist on trying to be superhuman, however, you will find that you're all too human as the wheels of your leadership vehicle come off due to stress, failure, or lack of followers.

Do what you must do to learn about who you are and aren't. Build on your strengths and minimize your weaknesses. Don't rely on charisma or special talents to prop up your leadership position. Work to know yourself and then improve from that base of knowledge.

In the next section, let's take a look at another biblical hero. I've studied Daniel's leadership for some time and would like to share with you some of what I've learned from that man.

Section Six

THE PRICE OF LEADERSHIP FOR DANIEL

*This man Daniel was found to have a keen mind
and knowledge and understanding,
and also the ability to interpret dreams, explain riddles,
and solve difficult problems*
(Daniel 5:12).

Chapter Nineteen

THE AGONY OF VICTORY

Do you remember the opening of the classic Saturday afternoon TV sports show on ABC called "The Wide World of Sports"? The announcer would introduce the show by saying, "The thrill of victory..." as we watched a clip of some heroic sports deed. He would then say "The agony of defeat..." and a skier would careen off a ski jump, bouncing off the ground as his goggles and equipment went flying.

In this chapter, I want to talk about the agony of victory. It's hard to be a successful leader, and it's a 24/7 job (24 hours a day/seven days a week) with crowds cheering a winning strategy or new product release. As we saw in both Moses' and David's life, there is often agony in victory for any leader, and Daniel, our focus for this section, was no exception.

In 1990, I began to work in Florida prisons and jails as a volunteer chaplain. I would go into the compounds at least once a week to lead Bible studies and visit with the men and women who were incarcerated. It was a learning experience, one that taught me a lot about our penal system and its residents and employees.

It was always a challenge to bring something relevant to a world that was as foreign to me as another nation. I learned that prisons had their own culture, currency (often illegal and black market), language, and social order. Most compounds had their own chapel with a full-time staff, and I found churches there with some committed Christians as members. It was indeed a different world than I expected.

While I was involved there, I began to search the Bible for examples that the inmates could relate to. That search led me to study Daniel, and he became my model prisoner for modern prisoners to study. While studying him in that context, I came to appreciate him as a leader who has something to say to you and me.

Daniel was a young man when the nation of Israel became embroiled in a military dispute with King Nebuchadnezzar of Babylon. Nebuchadnezzar won and Israel lost. The terms of victory were that some of the young men of Israel would be taken from Israel to Babylon to serve in King Nebuchadnezzar's royal court.

Then the king [Nebuchadnezzar] *ordered Ashpenaz, chief of his court officials, to bring in some of the Israelites from the royal family and the nobility— young men without any physical defect, handsome, showing aptitude for every kind of learning, well informed, quick to understand, and qualified to serve in the king's palace. He was to teach them the language and literature of the Babylonians. The king assigned them a daily amount of food and wine from the king's table. They were to be trained for three years, and after that they were to enter the king's service* (Daniel 1:3-5).

Daniel was among those chosen, so we know that he met the standards and was handsome, smart, born in the royal family, and had good leadership potential. Off he went to Babylon to learn a new culture and language—and that's how I related Daniel to the inmates I worked with. Daniel is a model Old Testament prisoner in Babylon.

Daniel became a leader in Babylon, but what a price he paid. He was taken from his homeland, forced to learn new customs, and expected to learn a new religion. He went to school (there's the price of education again) and was eventually appointed to be head of the wise men of Babylon, a nation known for its multiplicity of gods and religious traditions. All this must have been an incredibly difficult situation for a young Jewish man accustomed to worshipping one God in the comfort of his own culture in Israel.

We are told that Daniel was a wise man. When King Nebuchadnezzar had a dream, he ordered the wise men in Babylon to interpret the dream, although he refused to tell them what the dream was! They all said it was impossible, but not Daniel. The Bible tells us that he "went in to the king and asked for time, so that he might interpret the dream for him" (Daniel 2:16). During the night, Daniel had a vision that enabled him to interpret the dream.

Daniel responded to God's help with the following prayer:

Praise be to the name of God for ever and ever; wisdom *and power are his. He changes times and seasons; he sets up kings and deposes them. He gives* wisdom *to the* wise *and knowledge to the discerning. He reveals deep and hidden things; he knows what lies in darkness, and light dwells with him. I thank and praise you, O God of my fathers: You have given me* wisdom *and power, you have made known to me what we asked of you, you have made known to us the dream of the king"* (Daniel 2:20-23 emphasis added).

Earlier I referred to wisdom as a component that is absolutely necessary for any leader. In *Vine's Dictionary of Old and New Testament Words,* wisdom is defined as "prudence in the management of affairs." *Webster's Dictionary* defines wisdom as "following the soundest course of action, based on knowledge, experience, understanding, etc."

Daniel would have preferred to deliver his wisdom back home in Israel, but would he have been as wise there as he was in Babylon? Often a leader must go where there is no wisdom, where the need for leadership is so desperate that his or her impact will be greatest. That was Daniel's price for leadership. He was put in a place where his suffering and pain added to his body of knowledge, which in turn added a special dimension to his wisdom. He had divine help in obtaining wisdom, and he changed the course of Babylonian history. That's what wisdom can do.

Daniel had a story to tell based on what happened to him. He led the wise men of Babylon, and I think he told his story to them. That's what leaders do. Things happen to them that help shape their values. These experiences add a depth that allows them not only to lead others, but also to form and shape others into better leaders. Their experiences give them a body of wisdom that teaches others by example and, where appropriate, by actual teaching or classroom settings.

Noel Tichy, professor at the University of Michigan, consultant and author, writes about what he calls the teachable point of view in his book, *The Leadership Engine.* Tichy points out that successful leaders reproduce other leaders through what he calls a teachable point of view. Every leader needs to have the ability to impart what his or her values are and how they were developed. Tichy writes,

> Teaching is at the heart of leading. In fact, it is through teaching that leaders lead others. Leading is not dictating specific behavior. It is not issuing orders and commanding compliance. Leading is getting others to see a situation as it really is and to understand what responses need to be taken so that they will act in ways that will move the organization toward where it needs to be. Whether it is teaching something as simple as what concrete tasks need to take precedence over others this week, or something as complex as how to make good decisions, teaching is how ideas and values get transmitted. Therefore, in order to be a leader at any level of an organization, a person must be a teacher. Simply put, if you aren't teaching, you aren't leading.[30]

Daniel was a great teacher, and that made him a great leader. I'm not sure just how much actual or formal teaching he did in his day, but his life story has been reproduced and read by countless millions down through the ages. What Daniel did became a matter of "public record," and many leaders have learned from his wisdom and experience. If no one else has benefited, I certainly have. And I have to believe that many inmates who studied Daniel with me learned from him as well.

Tichy relates examples of great leaders who were or are great teachers. They translate their wisdom into action not only through business plans and profits, or through larger churches or more communities transformed, but also through a systematic and clear sharing of the truths that they hold dear. He points to leaders such as Jack Welch, CEO of General Electric, who spends 30% of his time teaching his employees and business leaders; and John Maxwell, who pastored a church in San Diego but today from his base in Atlanta teaches leadership principles to pastors and non-pastors alike.

Just look at the number of books written by leaders. They help the writer clarify his or her "teachable point of view." Someone once said that one writes to see what one thinks and to clarify the same. It works for me. My writing and seminars are part of my leadership as I attempt to motivate, train, and instruct leaders out of the wisdom and experience I have gained over the years.

Did Daniel write? I think he wrote the book of Daniel that carries his name. In that book, he shared with all of us the agony that went with his victory. He was a man of wisdom because he took what happened to him and turned it all into a comprehensive story of how to succeed and stay true to yourself.

Who are you teaching? What are you doing to preserve the stories that are making you the leader you are or will be? I developed my *Life Is a Gold Mine* seminar in 1985 before I ever taught my first workshop and long before my book was written. I didn't know what I would do with the material, but I felt I had to capture the essence of who I was and what I had been through. I encourage you to do the same.

What good is wisdom and experience if you can't share it with anyone? Why go through tough times for you and you alone? Doesn't it make perfect sense to share what you have agonized over with someone else, perhaps saving them the pain of what you've been through or showing them there is gain in their pain?

The price of leadership for Daniel was wisdom, and that comes only from experiences that teach. He took that wisdom and taught others. If you'll do the same, you'll enhance your leadership and make sure that there are others who will build on what you've learned. You'll be able to teach others what you learned out of the agony of victory.

Chapter Twenty

A MAN OF INTEGRITY

The newspaper is full of stories about leaders who lack integrity—men and women who, while leading, had some breach of trust that usually led to personal gain. Even the president of the United States, as of the writing of this book, has been found guilty, although society's ambivalence about the issue of morals and ethics allowed him to stay in office.

I've repeatedly stated that leaders aren't perfect people; neither are their followers. We'll never have perfect leaders. Integrity doesn't require perfection, however. Rather, integrity demands that leaders and followers take responsibility for wrongs done and take steps to correct or make restitution for those wrongs.

Dr. Robert Clinton talks about what he calls the integrity check in his book entitled *The Making of a Leader*. He writes:

> At the heart of any assessment of biblical qualifica-
> tions for leadership lies the concept of integrity—that
> uncompromising adherence to a code of moral, artistic,
> or other values that reveals itself in sincerity, honesty,
> and candor and avoids deception or artificiality. The

God-given capacity to lead has two parts: giftedness and character. Integrity is at the heart of character.[31]

Dr. Clinton goes on to discuss the "integrity check," and uses Daniel as an example. Please bear with this long passage, but I believe it says best what needs to be said in this chapter:

An emerging leader becomes aware of the importance of integrity through integrity checks. An *integrity check* is a test that God uses to evaluate intentions in order to shape character. This check is a springboard to an expanded sphere of influence. There are three parts to an integrity check: the challenge to consistency with inner convictions, the response to the challenge, and the resulting expansion of ministry [or leadership].

In Daniel 1:8-21, Daniel faced an integrity check that could have cost him his life.

But Daniel resolved not to defile himself with the royal food and wine, and he asked the chief official for permission not to defile himself this way. Now God had caused the official to show favor and sympathy to Daniel, but the official told Daniel, "I am afraid of my lord the king, who has assigned you food and drink. Why should he see you looking worse than the other young men your age? The king would then have my head because of you."

Daniel then said to the guard whom the chief official had appointed over Daniel, Hananiah, Mishael and Azariah, "Please test your servants for ten days: Give us nothing but vegetables to eat and water to drink. Then compare our appearance with that of the young men who eat the royal food, and treat your servants in accordance with what you see." So he agreed to this and tested them for ten days.

At the end of the ten days they looked healthier and better nourished than any of the young men who ate the royal food. So the guard took away their choice food and the wine they were to drink and gave them vegetables instead.

To these four young men God gave knowledge and understanding of all kinds of literature and learning. And Daniel could understand visions and dreams of all kinds.

At the end of the time set by the king to bring them in, the chief official presented them to Nebuchadnezzar. The king talked with them, and he found none equal to Daniel, Hananiah, Mishael and Azariah; so they entered the king's service. In every matter of wisdom and understanding about which the king questioned them, he found them ten times better than all the magicians and enchanters in his whole kingdom. Daniel remained there until the first year of King Cyrus.[32]

Dr. Clinton offers this explanation of this incident:

Daniel, a teenager away from home and parental influence, was forced to decide if the convictions he grew up with were his own. In this case the *inner conviction* was a religious one involving food. He was under pressure to violate this conviction, but he stuck to his conviction *(response)*. God gave him relationships that allowed him to work out a plan that did not compromise his convictions. God honored his unyielding character. Daniel and his friends were respected for their knowledge and skills and were given top-level government jobs. This promotion to a strategic position is an example of *expansion*—the third element of an integrity check. Daniel stood firm and saw God provide a solution. This enabled him to stand on even tougher issues later in life. All three elements of the integrity check are found in this passage.[33]

Daniel had values-based integrity that helped him make decisions. He decided to be true to the dietary laws of his God and people in Babylon. His integrity didn't cost him his leadership; his integrity enhanced his leadership. He was a man of integrity.

Stephen Covey writes in *The 7 Habits of Highly Effective People* about the need to build an "Emotional Bank Account" with people. Deposits, he points out, are made through courtesy, kindness, honesty, and keeping commitments.

> Lack of integrity can undermine almost any other effort to create high trust accounts. People can seek to understand, remember the little things, keep their promises, clarify and fulfill expectations, and still fail to build reserves of trust if they are inwardly duplicitous.

> Integrity includes but goes beyond honesty. Honesty is telling the truth—in other words, *conforming our words to reality*. Integrity is *conforming reality to our words*—in other words, keeping promises and fulfilling expectations. This requires an integrated character, a oneness, primarily with self but also with life.[34]

Integrity is a vital price of leadership for anyone who is serious about establishing a leadership style and legacy that will impact the world in a positive manner. Daniel's actions, not only in the instance above but also throughout his career, still speak today of a man who had a clear understanding of what it meant to be a man of integrity. He didn't talk about it; he operated in it.

Later in his career, there were many people who were jealous of Daniel's high position and sought to bring him down. When they observed him at work, we find this testimony to his level of integrity that didn't wane as the years went on.

> *Now Daniel so distinguished himself among the administrators and the satraps by his exceptional qualities that the king planned to set him over the whole kingdom. At this, the administrators and satraps tried to find grounds for charges against Daniel in his conduct of government affairs, but they were unable to do so. They could find no corruption in him, because he was trustworthy and neither corrupt nor negligent. Finally, these men said, "We will never find any basis for charges against this man Daniel unless it has something to do with the law of his God"* (Daniel 6:3-5).

It's my hope that if a group of detractors observed me, they would have to come to the same conclusion. That's part of the price of leadership—to be above reproach. If a mistake is made, then integrity demands that a leader take ownership for it and make it right. In this generation where everyone is a victim and wrongs done seem to be no one's fault, there's a desperate need for men and women of integrity to lead the way.

Perhaps you are an emerging leader and find yourself in the midst of what Dr. Clinton referred to as an integrity check. Or maybe you're an established leader who finds opportunities for your integrity to weaken. In either case, I urge you to hold on to your values. Make decisions that are consistent with who you are and what you believe. Don't sell out or cut corners hoping that no one is watching. That's not the way to become or remain a leader.

Daniel was a man of integrity. His leadership remains a model to follow 2,500 years after he led. You might say his leadership has survived the test of time. I want mine to do the same, and I'm willing to pay the price of leadership that demands integrity. May God help me, and you, to pay that price.

Chapter Twenty-One

IF

I've often said in my purpose seminars that I've never looked for a job in my adult life. I don't have a resumé and have never conducted a job search. When I've been unemployed, the phone has rung, and someone has asked me to take over some position. I wish I could say that every transition has been an easy one. Unfortunately, it's a difficult thing for me, and I believe for other leaders, to step out of a particular place of leadership once you're a leader.

Someone has said that the best leaders are ones who also know how to follow. I can identify with anyone who follows, for I've done my share. I can relate to anyone who questions my leadership decisions, and I have lots of grace for a disgruntled follower. I may have to help that follower find another leader to follow, but I still have grace for where they are and what they're going through.

Daniel was a good follower, and I think he knew how to step out of leadership gracefully after having enjoyed a leadership position. Part of the price of leadership is to not hold onto your leadership position too tightly. Otherwise, you may find yourself defending the top of your hill when it's really time to retreat and find another hill. I've counseled many leaders that the time to quit is when they're on top. If you do, someone may give you a lamp as a going-away present. If you wait too long, those same people may throw the lamp at you as you walk out the door!

Daniel had a distinguished career serving King Nebuchadnezzar. When the king died, as all leaders eventually do, his son Belshazzar took over for him. We read in Daniel 5 that this son threw a drinking party for his friends, using the drinking utensils that his father had taken from Daniel's Israel. As Belshazzar and his friends drank, "they praised the gods of gold and silver, of bronze, iron, wood and stone" (Daniel 5:4).

Their party was interrupted by an unexpected visitor.

Suddenly the fingers of a human hand appeared and wrote on the plaster of the wall, near the lampstand in the royal palace. The king watched the hand as it wrote. His face turned pale and he was so frightened that his knees knocked together and his legs gave way (Daniel 5:5-6).

So what did the king do? He called for all the wise men of Babylon and offered a large reward to anyone who could interpret the words that were written on the wall. All the wise men came, but no one could interpret the handwriting. As the king panicked, the queen came in and gave him some advice.

The queen, hearing the voices of the king and his nobles, came into the banquet hall. "O king, live forever!" she said. . . . "There is a man in your kingdom who has the spirit of the holy gods in him. In the time of your father he was found to have insight and intelligence and wisdom like that of the gods. King

If

Nebuchadnezzar your father . . . appointed him chief of the magicians . . . Call for Daniel, and he will tell you what the writing means" (Daniel 5:10-12).

Now I ask you, where was Daniel? Why wasn't he already serving in the king's court? I believe that this new king removed Daniel from his position of leadership to make room for his own friends and advisers. The queen had to tell Belshazzar that Daniel even existed. Once the chief adviser under Nebuchadnezzar, Daniel was now in semi-retirement in some Babylonian assisted-living facility!

Daniel was a gracious man who didn't hold onto his leadership too tightly. He was able to go with the flow of promotion and demotion, the ebb and flow of leadership. When summoned to the king, Daniel came. Belshazzar offered him a large reward for interpreting the writing on the wall.

Now Daniel could have said, "Look, you fired me when you took over as king. You didn't think you needed me, and now you call me when you're in trouble. I see that you're also using the drinking utensils that you stole from my nation when you brought me here. So I'm not going to interpret anything for you. Figure it out for yourself!"

Part of the price of leadership is to look past the insults, the oversights, and the inequities in order to lead when the need arises and the door opens. That's what Daniel did.

Then Daniel answered the king, "You may keep your gifts for yourself and give your rewards to someone else. Nevertheless, I will read the writing for the king and tell him what it means" (Daniel 5:17). Daniel did just that and told the king the bad news that the days of his kingly reign were ended. That night, Belshazzar was assassinated! When the new king took over, he promoted Daniel back to his original position.

The more I lead, the less anxious I am to do so. I know I'm a leader, but sometimes I have to take a back seat and humble myself. Humility is a good trait for any leader to have, because it keeps the leader from having too high an opinion of his or her leadership. If you're willing to give up your leadership, you won't protect it at any cost. It keeps you from being corrupted by the power that comes with leadership. That can spare you, your followers, and the organization you're leading from a lot of pain.

I've had to walk away from more than a few leadership positions. Some of those transitions have been painful. I've tried in each case to make it easy for that to happen, to not let a power struggle occur. I've tried not to let followers sympathize with me to the point that they couldn't follow the leader who replaced me. Finally, I've tried to stay on good terms with those who remained behind, offering my help and services if they were asked for (but then and only then).

I carry in my planner a poem by Rudyard Kipling entitled "IF." I'm not a big fan of poetry, but this poem has impacted my life and leadership.

> If you can keep your head when all about you
>   Are losing theirs and blaming it on you;
> If you can trust yourself when all men doubt you,
>   But make allowance for their doubting, too;
> If you can wait and not be tired by waiting,
>   Or being lied about, don't deal in lies;
> Or being hated don't give way to hating
>   And yet don't look too good, nor talk too wise;
> If you can dream—and not make dreams your master;
>   If you can think—and not make thoughts your aim,
> If you can meet with Triumph and Disaster

If

And treat those two imposters just the same;
If you can bear to hear the truth you've spoken
　Twisted by knaves to make a trap for fools,
Or watch the things you gave your life to broken,
　And stoop and build 'em up with worn-out tools:
If you can make one heap of all your winnings
　And risk it on one turn of pitch-and-toss,
And lose, and start again at your beginnings
　And never breathe a word about your loss;
If you can force your heart and nerve and sinew
　To serve your turn long after they are gone,
And so hold on when there is nothing in you
　Except the Will which says to them 'Hold on!'
If you can talk with crowds and keep your virtue,
　Or walk with Kings—nor lose the common touch,
If neither foes nor loving friends can hurt you,
　If all men count with you, but none too much;
If you can fill the unforgiving minute
　With sixty seconds' worth of distance run,
Yours is the Earth and everything that's in it,
　And—which is more—you'll be a Man, my son!

I love the line that says, "If you can meet Triumph and Disaster and treat those two imposters just the same." I'm never as good or as bad as I think I am when I'm leading. Success in leadership can be fleeting and can quickly turn into a temporary, if not permanent, failure. If I can keep that in mind, it will help me keep a proper perspective on what's happening around me.

I also appreciate the picture painted by the phrase, "If you can make one heap of all your winnings and risk it on one turn of pitch-and-toss, and lose, and start again at your beginnings and never breathe a word about your loss." There's risk involved in leadership, and sometimes the risk doesn't pan out as expected. But if I, as a leader, stop risking because I'm afraid of losing my "high position" or pension, then I've stopped being an effective leader. I'm not for reckless decisions, but I am for calculated risk that can lead to greater gain for followers and the organization I'm leading.

The price of leadership for Daniel was:

- Wisdom from experience
- Integrity
- Loss of leadership

As we close this study of leadership, I hope you've gained some new insights that will help you to become a better and more effective leader. I hope you realize that just because you're called a leader doesn't mean you're providing leadership to those around you. Leadership can come from anyone whether they're called "leader" or not because those who serve, communicate, train, and build a team are the real leaders in any situation regardless of their title or salary.

I want to be remembered as a good leader who helped others be the same. I offer this book to all who seek the same objective. Together let's impact our generation for good and take leadership to new levels of excellence. Let's pay the price to be leaders whom God can use and people can follow.

NOTES

Section One

[1] Robert K. Greenleaf, *On Becoming a Servant-Leader* (San Francisco: Jossey-Bass Publishers, 1996), pages 144-45.

[2] *Ibid.*, page 289.

[3] Warren Bennis, *Co-Leaders: The Power of Great Partnerships* (New York: John Wiley and Sons, Inc., 1999), page 4.

[4] Max DePree, *Leadership Is an Art* (New York: Dell Publishing, 1989), page 11.

[5] Robert K. Greenleaf, *Servant Leadership* (New York: Paulist Press, 1977), page 13.

[6] Larry C. Spear, editor, *Insights on Leadership* (New York: John Wiley and Sons, Inc., 1998), page 23.

[7] *Ibid.*, page 25.

[8] Anonymous

[9] Robert K. Greenleaf, *On Becoming a Servant-Leader* (San Francisco: Jossey-Bass Publishers, 1996), page 129.

[10] *Ibid.*, page 129.

[11] *Ibid.*, page 140.

Section Two

[12] Stephen R. Covey, *The 7 Habits of Highly Effective People* (New York: Simon and Schuster Inc., 1989), pages 18-19.

Section Three

[13] Larry C. Spear, editor, *Insights on Leadership* (New York: John Wiley and Sons, Inc., 1998), pages 22-23.

[14] *Ibid.*, page 23.

[15] John Haggai, *Lead On!* (Milton Keynes, England: Word Publishing, 1986), page 41.

[16] *Ibid.*, page 42.

[17] Peter F. Drucker, *Managing in a Time of Great Change* (New York: Truman Talley Books/Dutton, 1995), pages 32-33.

[18] Robert K. Greenleaf, *Servant Leadership* (New York: Paulist Press, 1977), page 19.

Section Five

[19] Peter F. Drucker, quoted from the Closing Plenary Session of the 1999 Leadership and Management Conference in Los Angeles, California, November 9, 1999.

[20] Alec MacKenzie, *The Time Trap* (New York: American Management Association, 1990), page 109.

[21] Merril E. and Donna N. Douglass, *Manage Your Time, Your Work, Yourself* (New York: American Management Association, 1993), page 109.

[22] Peter F. Drucker, *The Effective Executive* (New York: Harper and Row, 1966), page 35.

[23] *Ibid.*, page 27.

[24] *Ibid.*, page 49.

[25] *Ibid.*, page 49.

[26] *Ibid.*, page 51.

[27] Peter F. Drucker, *Management Challenges for the 21st Century* (New York: Harper Collins, 1999), page 164.

[28] *Ibid.,* pages 165-167.

[29] Peter F. Drucker, quoted from the Closing Plenary Session of the 1999 Leadership and Management Conference in Los Angeles, California, November 9, 1999.

Section Six

[30] Noel M. Tichy, *The Leadership Engine* (New York: Harper Collins, 1997), page 57.

[31] Dr. J. Robert Clinton, *The Making of a Leader* (Colorado Springs: NavPress, 1988), page 58.

[32] *Ibid.*, page 58.

[33] *Ibid.*, pages 59-60.

[34] Stephen R. Covey, *The 7 Habits of Highly Effective People* (New York: Simon and Schuster Inc., 1989), pages 195-196.

To book speaking engagements
or for information on other books and tapes, call or write:

GOLD MINE DEVELOPMENT CO.
Developing the gold in every individual

Dr. John W. Stanko, President
P.O. Box 91069 • Pittsburgh, PA 15221-7069
412-242-4448 • Fax: 412-242-6506
E-mail: johnstanko@purposequest.com
www.purposequest.com

Gold Mine Development Company's mission is to conduct seminars, produce publications, and provide other resources that will help you and/or your company identify your purpose, set appropriate goals, and order your life to accomplish what you were created to do. GMDC offers the following services:

- Motivational speaking
- Time management seminars
- Leadership coaching
- Life purpose seminars
- Staff profiling and evaluation
- Natural Church Development™ profiles
- Conference and event coordination

Other books by John Stanko:

Life Is a Gold Mine
Thousands of people around the world have been challenged by this book. It teaches you how to effectively and efficiently fulfill your life's mission.   ISBN 0-9637311-2-2 192 pg. PB $11.95

I Wrote This Book on Purpose
In a humorous, penetrating style, John Stanko helps you sort through your life and determine what God's purpose is for you.
ISBN 1-58169-011-8 128 pg. PB $7.95

A Daily Dose of Proverbs
Here's a devotional that makes Proverbs come alive. With wit, humor, and candor, John Stanko illuminates the wisdom of Proverbs in the context of today's needs. ISBN# 0-9637311-8-1 376 pg. PB $14.95

Other books of interest to leaders:

A Gathering of Eagles by Col. Jimmie Dean Coy
More than 300 Medal of Honor recipients, ex-POWs, and military, political, and religious leaders share their core beliefs about leadership, success, and significance.
ISBN 1-58169-049-5 320 pg. PB $14.95

The Little Book of Business Wisdom by Brian Banashak
Business wisdom for the novice and veteran alike. Packed with 88 principles for success—each with Scripture verse and testimony.
ISBN 1-58169-041-X 96 pg. PB $5.95

Money and the Christian by Caleb McAfee
Would you like to earn more, save more and give more? Would you like to enjoy true financial freedom & debt-free living? This book shows you how!. ISBN 0-9656010-0-5 192 pg. 8.5" x 11" Softcover $14.95

Proverbs of Success by John Grogan
The heart and soul of highly effective people. John Grogan has been a professional trainer and speaker for over 30 years. This book captures the essence of the wisdom he has shared with audiences around the globe. ISBN 1-58169-045-2 96 pg. PB $5.95

Start Your Own Business by Caleb McAfee
A step-by-step guide to successfully starting and operating a profitable business based on biblical principles. It has helped countless people fulfill their dream of owning a successful business. ISBN 0-9656010-1-3 368 pg. 8.5" x 11" Soft. $24.95

Navigating Toward Home by Craig Peters
Using a nautical metaphor, Craig Peters helps men to chart a course toward biblical manhood. You'll learn how to balance your career and family life, etc. For individual or group study. ISBN 58169-047-9 192 pg. $10.95